UNSTOPPABLE FORCE
STRENGTH TRAINING FOR CLIMBING

BY: STEVE BECHTEL
AND
CHARLIE MANGANIELLO

UNSTOPPABLE FORCE
STRENGTH TRAINING FOR CLIMBING

Text © Steve Bechtel and Charlie Manganiello
Illustrations and Layout © Kian Stewart
Exercise Photos © Zach Snavely (Unless otherwise noted)

ISBN 978-1-7923-0503-0

Cover Photo © Ryan Ferrian

Climb Strong
134 Lincoln St.
Lander WY 82520
www.climbstrong.com

TABLE OF CONTENTS

"YOU ARE ABOUT TO WITNESS THE STRENGTH OF STREET KNOWLEDGE."

DR. DRE

CHAPTER 1

WELCOME TO STRENGTH

INTRODUCTION

"

HE FIRST TOLD IT TO ME WHEN I WAS A RUSTY GRAMMAR SCHOOL KID WHO'D JUST BEEN CONVINCED BY HIM TO COME OUT FOR THE TRACK TEAM AND WHO WANTED TO QUIT BECAUSE MY LEGS LOOKED LIKE STRAWS NEXT TO THE OTHER GUYS'.

'I'LL NEVER MAKE IT THIS YEAR, MR. RILEY,' I SAID TO HIM DEJECTEDLY.

'WHO SAYS WE'RE TRYING TO MAKE IT THIS YEAR?' HE ANSWERED. 'YOU'RE TRAINING FOR FOUR YEARS FROM NEXT FRIDAY, JESSE.'

IT WAS FINE IN HIGH SCHOOL WHEN I STARTED BREAKING RECORDS, EXCEPT THE TIME SOON CAME WHEN I COULDN'T IMPROVE ON MY PAST PERFORMANCES AND EVEN DROPPED DOWN A BIT. I WAS LIKE THE SHOW BUSINESS STAR WHO HAS NOTHING LEFT FOR AN ENCORE, WHO IS AFRAID OF TODAY BECAUSE OF YESTERDAY'S SUCCESS.

'WHERE DO I GO FROM HERE?' I FINALLY ASKED MR. RILEY.
'KEEP TRAINING.'

'FOR WHAT?'

"WHY FOR FOUR YEARS FROM FRIDAY, OF COURSE.'

I TOOK HIS ADVICE. FOUR YEARS FROM FRIDAY HAPPENED TO BE THE OLYMPICS."

JESSE OWENS, *BLACKTHINK*

We train athletes, coach group classes, consult with people looking to get stronger, and write about strength training week after week. We know it can be challenging to put together a plan that progresses toward your training and performance goals, but it doesn't have to be. The two biggest errors we see are:

1. Only giving a strength session a couple of tries before moving to the next one.

2. Lacking consistency throughout the entire year.

Strength training, in its purest form, can follow a pretty basic structure for an entire year and you'll still see progress. You could pick five exercises, vary the loads a bit, hit the gym for an hour or less a couple of days a week, and leave the year way ahead of where you started.

Why doesn't everyone do it? Because it's too easy. Athletes want the "expert" level session or they get bored with the routine. Guess what? Salad is boring too, but we all know it's good for us. It's the same with training strength. We know how to get you strong, you just have to put in the work and be very patient. There is no magic pill, the truth is that as long as you stick with the training, do a little bit over the long haul, it will happen. It's that simple.

In *Unstoppable Force - Strength Training For Climbers* we break strength training into its simplest facets and give you the tools you need to execute training in a hotel room while traveling for work, in your garage, or a fully operational weight room.

RULES OF STRENGTH TRAINING

1. KEEP IT SIMPLE.
There are plenty of complicated formulas to see results in strength training, but let's leave that to the very elite lifters. You need to push out of your comfort zone and need to do it regularly, but that's it.

2. YOU'LL HAVE A FOCUS IN YOUR TRAINING (I.E. PULL-UPS), BUT TRAIN ALL MAJOR MOVEMENT PATTERNS ALL THE TIME TOO.
The days of just "back" and "chest" day are long gone. We aren't bodybuilding, we are training to support rock climbing.

3. STICK WITH A TRAINING SESSION FOR TEN OR MORE SESSIONS BEFORE CHANGING.
If you switch too soon you'll miss out on ideal adaptation.

4. LEARN THE MOVEMENT CORRECTLY FIRST BEFORE YOU CONSIDER ADDING LOAD.
We want your body to handle little to light loads before we really start stressing it with heavy weight.

5. IF YOU CAN'T PERFORM THE EXERCISE, FIGURE OUT WHY.
Don't put strength on top of dysfunction. Look at range-of-motion, your base strength, and your technique before you go heavy. If you can't figure it out, a good strength coach will.

6. STRENGTH TRAINING IS NOT DONE INSTEAD OF CLIMBING, BUT IN ADDITION TO IT.
For the majority of us, there is no need to do strength training in just the off season. In-season sessions can be short and even marry in to climbing training sessions.

7. YOU WILL NOT GET HUGE.

Often, people are reluctant to lift weights because they think they will get "big." Although bodybuilding and strength training use the same tools, the methods are different. Hypertrophy is normally achieved by training with light to medium loads trained in high volumes. Picture a cyclist (large quads) or a swimmer (broad shoulders)...did this hypertrophy occur because of weight training?

8. LITTLE AND OFTEN OVER THE LONG TERM.

You don't need to kill it in your sessions, you just need to keep showing up and "coaxing" the gains.

9. DON'T CHASE THE PUMP.

Fitness is a result of what you did, not how it felt. Starting today, you need to stop judging your workouts by how you felt at the end of them, and instead compare performance to your previous numbers. This means you need to start keeping a training log.

10. TENSION IS KING.

The more tension your body can create and sustain, the better you can transfer power. This is the underlying goal of most of your training.

11. STRONG ANTAGONISTS MAKE STRONG AGONISTS.

Many athletes have created large imbalances in their musculature. If one movement (such as pull-ups) substantially overpowers the opposite (such as pressing), the primary movement can stop progressing, no matter how hard you train.

12. HAVE A REASON FOR EVERY EXERCISE YOU DO.

Every exercise, every session...you must be able to give a good "why." If you can't directly tie your exercise to better climbing, don't do it.

WHY DOES STRENGTH TRAINING HELP CLIMBERS?

Let's take a quick poll. Who thinks they will "bulk" up if they lifts weights? This is the biggest myth out there in weight training and it is crippling an athlete's potential every day they believe it. People need to know it's just not true. Go ahead, say it. It's not true. People used tell Schwarzenegger, "We don't want to look like you." His reply, "Don't worry, you never will."

The amount of food you have to consume and the volume of training needed to add a lot of muscle is more than most can handle or would ever want to do. We're talking about setting an alarm for 2am and choking down your eighth chicken cutlet of the day.

OK, say you do lift weights here and there, but are confused on what to do to get stronger. The confusion around volume and intensity is difficult to understand. If you want to get stronger the intensity needs to be high and the volume low. If you feel "the burn" you're either at a Zumba class, or doing too many reps at too low intensity to build real strength.

In strength, we keep the reps low and slowly increase loads. We want you to dial in the movement, stabilize surrounding joints, and be able to handle heavy loads later.

When lifting heavy we are taxing the central nervous system (CNS) and asking the body for more motor recruitment to handle the load. The more motor recruitment, the stronger we are. This is hard on the CNS and that's why we keep the volume low. In this book, we will help you define how to go heavy, how to correctly do the lifts, how much volume to pursue in different seasons, and how to get stronger on the rock. We will cover the most efficient and effective finger strength training protocols we know.

We all know climbing is very skill-specific and requires a massive amount of time practicing on the rock or at a local climbing gym. We will not go into climbing-specific practice, but we will talk about finger strength, core strength, and how these should be placed within the framework of your existing program. Climbers need to know that "just climbing" will only take them so far. By not gaining strength, you will not reach your full potential as an athlete. This book will help you get there.

We see strength training in every single sport. You could be training to be a 100m sprinter, going for the gold on the downhill course, or to be a top level beach volleyball player. The amount and degree of time in the weight room might differ from sport to sport, but it's still done year round by every elite athlete. The stronger you can be, the more efficient you are on the rock, and the better you can complete the skills of the sport.

We must also train strength to improve muscle imbalances and prevent injury. Climbers are awfully good at pulling, but can't press to save their lives. We have assessed climbers who could do a pull-up at 225lbs (125lbs bodyweight + 100lbs), but couldn't bench press 115lbs. This is a gaping hole in strength and must be addressed. The climber who doesn't address this weaknesses can end up with a shoulder injury or worse, will stop getting better! The body is smarter than our training habits. By having a really strong pull and such a weak press, the body will recognize this extreme imbalance and put a "governor" on the pull because it recognizes if it gets any strong the shoulder will be too over developed in one facet. Get your press stronger to pull stronger. Same goes for back and abs, same goes for quads and hamstrings.

We encourage you to put aside all the negative things you've heard about strength training , and learn how it can benefit your performance. We are not trying to get you to be the next best powerlifter, but we are here to get you better at the sport you love. Every athlete has to have some baseline of strength. We'll outline what is considered strong enough in major lifts. This is not news for most athletes, but it can be for climbers. This book can help you stop relying on "just climbing" and plug obvious leaks in the boat you call performance.

STRENGTH STANDARDS - HOW STRONG IS STRONG ENOUGH?

How do you know if you're strong enough? The easiest way is to do a global assessment of both general and specific measurements and look for major issues. Can you do a one-arm pull-up but not a single-leg squat? Can you deadhang an edge at bodyweight for 60 seconds, but fail to hold it for 5 pull-ups? We like assessments to address not only climbing-specific parameters, but general mobility, health, and the things that you're neurotic about, such as how big your legs are.

THE PROBLEM IS NOT TO FIND THE ANSWER, IT'S TO FACE THE ANSWER."

TERENCE MCKENNA

We also like the assessment to fit in one session. Your assessment should address where you are, but also where you want to be: if your endurance sucks, you don't necessarily need to train it if your goal this year is a 3-move boulder (On a related note, you might consider limiting your improvement goals to 1 or 2 qualities.). An assessment will give you a picture of a dozen ways you could be better. Getting better at one thing and not losing ground in the others over the next 3 months is, well, really good.

A GOOD PERSONAL ASSESSMENT HAS FOUR MAIN FACTORS:

1. General Health
2. Mobility
3. General Strength
4. Sport-Specific Conditioning

The first thing climbers like to assess is sport-specific stuff - am I sending or not? This is backward from where you should start, as the basics of health can bolster (or erode) everything you do in the sport. How is your cardiorespiratory system? We bash on climbers who run to get better at climbing, but hold that you should have the basic fitness to hike a couple of hours or go on an easy 30 minute run. We also feel you should be strong enough to fistfight an aid climber if necessary, but don't think it should be a regular part of your training. Is your body fat percentage in the healthy zone? Are you eating well? Are you sleeping enough? All of these "easys" are the foundation for doing the hard stuff.

A GOOD ASSESSMENT STARTS WITH MEASUREMENTS:

FOREARM GIRTH LEFT AND RIGHT - Are you losing mass there? If so, fix it.

WAIST CIRCUMFERENCE AT THE NAVEL - If this trends upward more than 1" in a year, your training goals just changed.

BODYWEIGHT - Getting heavier offseason is OK, but you should have a "line in the sand." Again, cross this line and your priority has to be to get back south of it. Unexplained weight gain is a real health concern, and is worth a trip to the doctor.

OTHER MEASUREMENTS - We test quad circumference in athletes that fear leg bulk, shoulder girth in some, etc.

Mobility is very individual, but a basic set of three measures is great for 90% of us.

THE FMS SHOULDER MOBILITY TEST will screen you for general mobility and left/right imbalance. If you are close to hand-length on both sides, maintenance here is fine. If you are much beyond that, a focused mobility program might be in order. You can find a local Functional Movement Screen specialist with a quick internet search.

OVERHEAD SQUAT WITH A PVC OR DOWEL. This test will tell you a lot about hip mobility and balance. If you can't keep your heels on the ground when squatting below parallel in this move, your hips are too tight, which also means your turnout probably sucks. The fix? Get some help from a qualified coach.

SPLITS. We like splits because you can tell everything about lower-limb flexibility by watching them. If you get as far into the splits as you can and could still swing a kettlebell, it might be worth improving them. If you just love doing the splits at every opportunity and your default Instagram pose is the natarajasana, you should deadlift more and toss the flexibility training.

NEXT, WE ASSESS ABILITIES:

Strength should not be looked at as absolutes as much as relationships between the basic movements. A huge discrepancy between your pulling and pushing muscles can mean injury, but it can also mean inhibition of gains in the stronger group. We get a lot of resistance from some climbers (get it ?!?) when it comes to weight training, but it's like investing in your retirement account... when you finally realize you need it, you wish you'd started years before. Our tests:

90 SECOND PLANK - If you can't do this, you need to squat and hinge. We only use the standard plank as a test, never as training. For most of us, it's just not hard enough to make us stronger.

2 REP PULL-UP - You can lie about one, but two reveals all. Men should be able to do BW + ½ , women BW + 1/3. This means if you are a 120 pound female, you should be able to do a pull-up with an additional 40 pounds added. Most rock climbers and boulderers can do this easily...which leads us to the obvious: maybe more pulling is not what we need. Also, if you can't rest your Adam's Apple on the bar at the top, it's not a pull-up.

VERTICAL JUMP - Test this one whenever you like. If it drops off from baseline, you might be overtraining. If it goes up after a particular phase of training, remember to do that training phase again soon! Hip extension in the vertical jump is the same movement as you do when you deadpoint, so get good at it.

1 MINUTE PUSH-UP TEST - This is a general upper body endurance test that tells us a lot. Over 30 is pretty good.

1 MINUTE INVERTED ROW - We do this on a TRX or rings, and start with the body horizontal. Count only reps where the wrists touch the sides of the ribs.

GRIP STRENGTH LEFT AND RIGHT. Look for slow steady improvements over time. This number traditionally doesn't correlate with higher grades on the rock, but it correlates well with general fitness and strength. Males should aim to hit above 3/4 bodyweight, females above ⅔ bodyweight. Greater grip strength correlate with better performances in almost all strength exercises.

ANKLES TO BAR. Do them slowly, with no lame-ass kip. If you can't do 10, add 5 sets of however many you can do perfectly, 3 times per week.

FRONT LEVER. You can't do it. You should be able to. Aim for five good ones.

PISTOL SQUAT. Start with the less-strong leg. Test reps holding a 12-16kg kettlebell or dumbbell to help with balance. Over five is pretty good. If you can do more than five, look for a different training priority. This is a very sport-specific movement and can drastically improve your climbing.

20MM EDGE DEADHANG FOR TIME. This is the Zlagboard contest edge. Most climbers should be able to at least hang this edge for 10-15 seconds. If you can't, start your training here. Aim to improve this every cycle.

18-20MM EDGE MAX HANG. Weight it up. Test your max for 5-10 seconds. If this doesn't improve after a strength cycle, your program sucks.

SKILLED TESTS. THESE SHOULD ONLY BE TESTED IF YOU KNOW HOW TO DO THE LIFTS.

1-ARM OVERHEAD PRESS. Start with your less-strong side. Most strong males should be able to press close to half-bodyweight. If you are way off, but your pull-ups are good, you may be at risk of shoulder issues.

DEADLIFT. 2x bodyweight is a good goal for a male athlete... which is reasonably strong if you weigh 400 pounds. If you can do 5 front levers, don't worry about what you can deadlift. Look for improvement over the long haul, and consider testing your 3 rep max instead of your single.

TURKISH GET-UP. Over 1/3 bodyweight on both sides is pretty good.

BENCH PRESS. If you can't bench your bodyweight for 3 reps, you may be holding back your pulling strength.

Your assessments should go hand in hand with your training plan and training log. Don't have one of those? Well, don't complain about not getting anywhere if you don't have a map.

Naturally, your assessments will differ. The aim is to do a regular self-assessment and look for problems. Big, obvious things are easier and more important to fix than worrying about whether to train 5-second hangs or 7-second hangs in the half-crimp. The assessment log becomes a fascinating way to look at your career over time. Pair it with a list of the problems or routes you sent in that cycle, and all kinds of interesting things start popping up.

The most important takeaway is not what the assessments alone tells you. When you see really good performances on the rock, there are clues as to why that happened in your logs and tests. A 2x bodyweight deadlift means very little unless it is tied to better performance.

CHAPTER 2

A FEW WORDS ON TRAINING IN GENERAL

IT'S LIKE FIGHTING A GORILLA. YOU DON'T STOP WHEN YOU'RE TIRED; YOU STOP WHEN THE GORILLA IS TIRED."

ROBERT STRAUSS

Training is how we get better...at everything. From learning to walk, to washing our faces, to adding numbers, we learn through progressive application of habits and processes. We can improve quickly, at first, through experimentation and play; through random or widely varied activities. When we first are learning to climb, just climbing is by far the best way to progress. As we advance, however, the changes needed to progress become more acute, require more focused efforts, and come in smaller increments. This is where training begins.

Training is different from exercising. Training is clearly directed and every session has a purpose. The purpose of those sessions is not to get tired, but to build toward an overall long-term improvement in some facet of your climbing. Deciding to start training is, by necessity, a long-term commitment. If you are ready to turn a corner in your performance, stepping up to a real training program can make all the difference in the world.

There is no right or wrong way to train as long as our activity produces the desired result. Think about a typical marathon. Hundreds of runners complete the event, all of them using a different method to get there. If their goal was to complete the race, the plan worked. Likewise, all the runners who set a personal record at that race also trained somewhat differently. These athletes, too, can say that their plan was a good plan. As long as your training produces steady improvements, there is no reason to change.

Rob Sleamaker, author of Serious Training for Endurance Athletes, makes a nice analogy to making chili when it comes to designing your training program. He says that dozens of chili recipes are delicious, and they have similar ingredients...the quality of the result is simply how you put them together. What we will try to put forth in this book is the basic structure of a few plans that have been effective for real rock climbers, not just programs reworked from another sport. We try to keep the theoretical out of our programs.

Our training must always start from the point of an honest needs assessment. What do I really need to do to get better? Do I really have weak fingers, or is it bad technique that's costing me? Is my endurance bad, or am I just afraid?

Early on in a climbing career, almost any form of exercise or climbing can lead to improvement. As a climber's training age increases, though, demands placed on the system during training must be more and more specific in order for the athlete to develop. Eventually total training volume becomes limited, both by ability to recover and time available to train. For these reasons, and advanced climber's training requires more intense work, technical refinement, and higher-quality efforts in training. Bottom line: train harder, not longer.

GUIDELINES FOR EFFECTIVE TRAINING

As we have said before, training is different than just climbing. Training requires planning and structure, but most of all it requires a (sometimes fanatical) dedication to progress. A huge key to success is to look at what you are currently doing and determine whether it's working. Are you seeing the progress you expect? Are you seeing progress at all? Are you following the training plan you've created, or are you falling back on old habits? Below, we've outlined a few things that we think are critical pre-training components for setting yourself up for successful training.

GET CHECKED OUT

It seems a little silly to athletic people to go get the OK from a doctor to begin training (you should probably get a doctor's OK to not train), but you can get some valuable information. A physical and a full blood workup can give you good information on how much you should be training, if you need supplements, and if you have any big problems looming on the horizon.

This is especially important if you've had physical issues in the past or if you've had bad experiences with heavy training. Boulderers who are overweight or are constantly fighting weight gain can sometimes pinpoint problems with a simple blood profile. We've seen many climbers who were being held back by a simple deficiency in a vitamin or mineral. If nothing else, having your health "confirmed" is worth the trip.

SET A BASELINE

Where are you starting, really? Effective training can be judged only on the results it produces. Just because the workouts in your new plan are difficult doesn't mean they are leading toward your goal. You have to know your starting point to tell if you're going anywhere. Do some basic testing as simple as assessing your performance on 3-5 limit level boulder problems, a few hard grips on the hangboard, and do a hard day of redpointing before starting a plan and see how it worked. You should also pick some pure strength tests, possibly some body girth measurements, and your bodyweight, such as the ones mentioned earlier. These same tests should be performed at the end of each training block.

Consider doing a finger strength max test (as outlined later in the book) once a month during strength cycles to assure your hard work is producing the desired results.

PLAN THE WORK, WORK THE PLAN

It doesn't matter how good the plan is if you don't follow it. Start with the simplest training plan you can, and follow it to the letter. If this means "boulder three times per week" then that's all you're going to have to do. In this book we offer several different training plans. We think every climber should start simple, adding more complex elements only as progress levels off.

No matter what, you need to follow a plan through to its end. We see athletes fail to complete training plans season after season, and the results are what you'd expect. In advanced plans, it's really rare to see any gain until the last week or two of a training block. If you never get there, guess what?

THINK LONG TERM

We all want to get better and get better fast. Effective training plans can sometimes provide quick results, but should always deliver long-term results. You're going to be a climber for a long time, especially if you take care of your body. Thinking long term means taking some layoffs each year, maybe 2-4 weeks without climbing. It means working on developing strength and endurance over season after season. It means allowing injuries to heal fully,

even if it means a year away from the rock. It means being patient with your training, especially as you reach closer to your potential.

It's abundantly clear that experience means more than conditioning. Build skills and strength and you can be assured you'll keep getting better for years to come. Getting to a high level of strength can require a lot of hard hours in the gym, but maintaining these gains is relatively easy. Never let yourself drop off too far from strength levels that you worked hard to achieve.

BRING IN A COACH OR TRAINING PARTNER

We are masters of sticking with the things at which we excel. Big, strong guys with crap technique love the dynos. Short people love lowball traverses. Steve has big hands and no power so he absolutely loves climbing at Maple Canyon. Does it make him better at his weaknesses? Not remotely.

What you need to find is a way to always check in against what is really holding you back. The easiest thing to do is ask a friend. Hire a coach - there are a ton out there and more popping onto the scene each year. Even the worst coach can pick up movement issues. Can't afford an expert? Videoing yourself is an effective way of catching and improving errors in movement. In fact, simply knowing that someone is watching has been shown to improve an athlete's quality of movement.

Training partners can really help with motivation. Getting in with like-minded and driven partners can really advance a career. The intensity of a group session can really push you, and you might see great gains in a short time. However...

BE WILLING TO TRAIN ALONE

You won't always have your good friends or significant other to climb with. If you're going to see real progress on your own training program, you're going to have to go it alone sometimes. For the most part, your hangboard workouts, endurance workouts, and even power endurance sessions will (and should) be done alone. Rarely do two climbers have the exact same needs and, thus, training plan.

You simply can't depend on others to carry you. Figure out what it's going to take to get you on the hangboard on the day you need to do it. Watch out for excuses...these are the things you use to avoid progress.

PROGRESS SLOWLY AT FIRST

Don't be fooled; there are no prodigies. Every top level climber out there from seasoned veterans to hardcore pre-teen sendmasters have put their time in. Climb a lot. Train starting from where you really are, not where you think you ought to be (or where you once were). Related to the tip above, you might spend a large portion of time alone in the gym until you get strong enough to train with others.

The faster one progresses through the grades, the less persistent his abilities. What this means is that the more like a pyramid your advancement looks (as opposed to a ladder) the more stable those abilities will become. In strength training, this is often called grinding; practicing the basics over and over until you own that level of ability.

In route climbing, we often see the wheels come off when a climber (in the U.S.) reaches the threshold grades such as 12a, 13a, 14a, etc. Instead of being content to work and "own" the d grades below them, they get obsessed with the new number, and reach too far. Luckily, bouldering follows a more logical scale, where the grades can be progressed step-wise, which is easier on the psyche.

TECHNICAL CORRECTNESS

At the edge of our fitness, skills decline. When you are pumped, you climb like crap. This is true throughout your training. Since climbing is a skill sport and requires careful technical movement, you must be careful to avoid learning bad motor patterns. How do we learn bad motor patterns? By doing familiar movements under a state of fatigue.

In your strength training and in your climbing, always stop the sets when you feel your form failing. This dedication to doing things right will benefit you more than your hard-earned pump every time.

THE FIRST RULE IS TO AVOID INJURY

Don't get hurt training. Just don't. In all our years of coaching, the worst injuries in our athletes occur when training. Not just training, but training without a proper warm-up or with improper form. Don't push it if you're feeling "a little something" in a finger or an elbow. Don't train if you are tired from last time. Take care of the body at all times so the body can take care of you.

ALLOW YOUR LIFE TO HAPPEN

You know how it is...stuff comes up. Understanding that you just can't stick to the plan all the time is critical. We think you're doing really well if you hit 9 of 10 planned sessions. You're going to get sick. You're going to have bad weather. You're going to have times of low motivation. Accept it and move on.

It's OK to have a little time off now and then. The alarms should go off when you start getting worse at climbing. Until this happens, let climbing be what it's supposed to be - a part of your life.

RECOVER

More is not better. The right amount is the right amount. In training, you have got to look at recovery as a fundamental component that must be balanced against your training. This means taking recovery periods each week, each month, and each year. We like to see at least one full rest day each week, at least one three-day rest each month, and at least one two-week period each year when you don't train at all.

The harder you climb and the older you get, the more important rest will become.

FACETS OF FITNESS

"

AN ATHLETE NEEDS TO TRAIN FIRST TO BE FIT FOR TRAINING BEFORE TRAINING FOR COMPETITION."

THOMAS KURZ

QUALITIES

We all know that there are different ways we can be "in shape." An athlete can get stronger, faster, more accurate, or can recover more quickly. He can train the body to generate more power or increase its range of motion. Most importantly, there is almost no facet of performance that can't be trained and improved. The primary qualities we are interested in developing as climbers are as follows:

STRENGTH

The body's ability to generate force is called strength. This manifests itself in absolute ability to contract a muscle or hold a static position. This is the master quality and all other facets of climbing fitness are derivatives of strength. Strength can be displayed isometrically (holding a static position), concentrically (shortening the muscle under load), or eccentrically (allowing the muscle to lengthen under load). For climbing, we primarily train the muscles isometrically and concentrically.

POWER

Power is strength with a speed component. If strength is a pull-up, power is a dyno. Effective climbing training involves building strength and then learning to speed it up. We get strong fingers on the hangboard then make them powerful on the campus board. We get strong arms in the weight room, and then make them powerful by bouldering. Power is a close cousin to strength and is trained in a similar way. Rest periods, set lengths, and weekly frequency are somewhat interchangeable. It's possible, and appropriate, to train strength and power concurrently.

MUSCULAR ENDURANCE

We use terms like strength-endurance and power-endurance and anaerobic-endurance to describe longer efforts in climbing. All of these sub-qualities are dependent more on energy provided by metabolic processes in the body than on the ability of the muscle or nervous system to generate force. However, the ability to continually generate high-force contractions in the forearm can be improved through specific strength training.

A need for high levels of muscular endurance in climbing is almost exclusively limited to the forearm. We rarely see a significant level of fatigue associated with any other muscle group - the sport almost always allows sufficient recovery between high load efforts for most of the body's muscles. The good news here is that total body muscular endurance is one of many facets you probably don't have to train.

CARDIORESPIRATORY ENDURANCE

Cardiorespiratory endurance is having the ability to sustain long efforts of low-intensity activity. Athletes that develop a high level of this kind of endurance not only improve in their ability to go long durations at a steady pace, but they also can improve their ability to recover between hard bouts of exercise such as boulder problems or routes. That being said, many people equate a high level of cardiorespiratory or aerobic endurance with the ability to display good endurance on rock climbs. The relationship is not strong, and sport specific endurance (gained by climbing or doing total-body activities such as weight circuits) is a better choice for climbers than running, cycling, or swimming.

As mentioned above, if you can't sustain a mild aerobic training effort such as a 30 minute run or 60 minute steady-paced bike ride, it may be an indicator that you are lacking in basic fitness. At this point, it may be wise to build an aerobic base of fitness by adding some general activity to your climbing training plan.

MOBILITY

Mobility is the quality of having strength through a full range of motion. It is a combination of both flexibility and strength, and an ideally mobile person should be able to display strength in several planes of movements as well as at several joint angles. We train mobility instead of flexibility in the hips and shoulders especially, as those joints deal with very high training loads and are the most susceptible to becoming immobile through inactivity.

FLEXIBILITY

Flexibility is a quality of individual muscles and muscle groups that indicates their ability to move through a complete range of motion regardless of the ability to display force. Flexibility is a great quality to develop, but for climbers it must be built on a foundation of good mobility.

IF IT HURTS, DON'T DO IT

If a specific movement hurts, don't do it. This doesn't mean if it made you sore, don't do it. Being a bit uncomfortable under tension is what strength is all about. However, if you have throbbing hip pain from deadlifting, burning elbows from pull-ups, creaky knees from front squat, or radiating pain in the shoulder from the bench press, it may mean the exercise isn't right for you - or that your form isn't right. If you find yourself reading an example workout you want to start incorporating in your own training and it calls for pull-ups, but pull-ups hurt your elbows, don't do pull-ups.

No amount of toughness and suffering is worth creating a chronic injury. We suffer enough through all the other difficulties of sending projects, the grind of training, and other hiccups along the way. There is no need to add in another. If something hurts, within a normal movement pattern and range-of-motion it needs to either be addressed with physical therapy, mobility work, or a change in exercise. Sometimes certain movements just hurt. For example: Maybe push-ups hurt your wrist and you stay away from them when they are programmed. Have you ever tried doing a push-up on hex dumbbells or a floor press instead?

It's not always that simple. Different bodies occasionally require different training. Sometimes climbers with shoulder injuries find overhead pressing painful. In some cases, no amount of PT and mobility work is going to change that. That climber just doesn't overhead press anymore. This doesn't mean they don't press at all, it just changes what kind of pressing they get to do.

CHAPTER 3

TOOLS OF THE TRADE

We try to make our training plans as flexible as possible. We want our athletes to be able to get strong, no matter where they travel in the world or what facility they have available. There are, however, ideal tools. Below you'll find a list of tools you'll need to implement the training plans in this book effectively. For the most part, a well-stocked home gym can cost you less than a year's gym membership. If you don't wish to build a home training set-up, make sure your gym has all of the tools listed in the coming pages.

THE HANGBOARD

In the late 1980s a friend telephoned Steve from the local climbing shop, saying, "You've got to get down here and check out the climbing simulator we just got!"

Above the door to the ski-tuning shop was bolted a 3-foot wide chunk of plastic with different edges and pockets all over it and two palm-shaped grips at the ends. Although not the futuristic "simulator" he'd imagined, the Metolius Simulator - the first widely distributed training board for climbing - would forever change the way we got strong for climbing.

Hangboards are everywhere these days. Some are tiny, some take up as much space as a good-sized TV, and others easily strap to the top of your climbing pack. Carefully refined to train most of the grip-types we encounter in climbing, these tools allow us to sustain (and gain) strength between days at the crag.

What's even better is that the hangboard allows us to quantify our strength. If you can hang a smaller hold than last week, or move down one size, you're seeing progress. And progress is everything.

A good hangboard has a nice texture that allows for training even with thin skin. A good board has a variety of holds, is in a clean and well-lit space. A good board is well-anchored and ready for lots of abuse.

You'll want to have hold types that develop the grips you need in your home area, and develop the grips where you are weakest. A variety of edges and pockets are a good start. For pinch grip strength, we still like pinch blocks (described later). The way that boards are built and used still falls short for good pinch training.

THE IRON

If you're going to train, make sure you have the right tools. Part of getting better is getting stronger. In fact, any time you match up two athletes of equal skill, you can bet the stronger of the two will come out on top. How do you get strong? Move weight.

Climbers like to think that we can get strong enough through just climbing. Somewhere along the way, though, your potential for strength outpaces your ability to stimulate it with bodyweight exercises and sport movement alone. At this point, the best track forward is to pick up some weights.

You are going to need a barbell. You'll need a variety of kettlebells and dumbbells and a good, solid, pull-up bar. You'll need some boxes to step and jump on. A good gym will have all these tools and probably more. You can outfit a home gym relatively cheaply, or you can invest in a gym membership so you don't have to store the stuff. The only non-negotiable is that you have got to get access to the tools.

When climbing, we usually fall off because of what's happening between the elbow and the fingers, strength training gets the rest of the body stronger.

PHOTO: SAM LIGHTNER, JR.

OTHER TOOLS

FOAM ROLLER

The foam roller is an inexpensive and useful tool. We use it for a light self-massage before training, but it can also be used as a recovery tool for more engaged self-massage or as a prop for mobility work. Most gyms will have a few of these. They are widely available online, and though there are some with a lot of "special features," we like the really simple ones. On the cheap? Try using a 30-inch section of PVC pipe.

SUPERBANDS OR MONSTER BANDS

These thick elastic bands are just a bit longer than a shoulder-length sling. Available in a variety of thicknesses and widths, most climbers can get by with a ½" and a 1" band for the exercises in this book. We use these bands in activation exercises, in some mobility work, and as resistance or assistance in strength exercises.

SUSPENSION STRAPS

Best known by the brand name TRX, these tools are a pair of nylon straps with plastic handles on one end and an anchor system on the other. They can be fixed to the top of a door or to a pull-up bar, and can be used for core work, stability drills, or advanced bodyweight strength drills. You can use the TRX or even a set of gymnastic rings for all of the suspension exercises described later.

PINCH BLOCKS

As mentioned above, training the pinch grip in a finger strength session is best done with a simple block of wood attached to some weights. We use a single 2x6 block (1½" thick) for thin pinches and a doubled one (3" thick) for wider ones. An eye bolt and some webbing allow you to attach load. These are commercially available now, and some of the blocks are really nice. A great alternative is the Tension Block, a small training block with a piece of cord attached to it that allows for training pinches and several grip positions. These are really great for climbers who travel, have limited training space, or experience shoulder pain in the overhead position.

GRIPPERS

The spring-loaded gripper is still the best tool for building crushing grip strength. The Iron Mind "Captains of Crush" are the industry standard. Start with the lightest ones and work your way up - the higher numbered grippers are for seriously elite grip athletes. We use these tool in warm-ups, but they really shine in off-season strength programs when we try to de-focus our isometric finger strength efforts.

FIND A GYM OR BUILD YOUR OWN

PHOTO: MEI RATZ

As we mentioned above, you're going to want a gym that is convenient, accessible, and has all the tools you need for training. If a gym lacks a tool or two, you can probably make some adjustments and make it work. If you are looking at needing multiple gym memberships, buying some equipment might be the way to go. Depending on where you live, a gym membership will run $500 to $1000 per year. If you live in a small house and your weight gym also offers climbing, this might be worth it.

If you have the space at home, though, it doesn't take too long to recoup the membership cost. A good bouldering wall will cost you $2000 to $4000, and the hangboard and weights might only run another $1000. You could have it paid off in just a couple of years. It's not a decision you need to make right away, either. Budget a few buck a month toward training tools while still training at the gym. Once you have collected enough gear for a home gym, make the transition.

The real choice is where you'll be happiest training. Don't compromise when it comes to facility.

CHAPTER 4

ESSENTIALS OF SUCCESSFUL PROGRAMMING

PHOTO: MATT ENLOW

Climbers' experiences with training vary greatly. Some experience great results while others see little payout for their work in the gym. Most of us think we know what a good workout feels like - a tiredness in the muscles, a general fatigue after training, and possibly soreness the next day. So how can we experience all of these things and still not progress in the sport?

The difficulty with judging the effectiveness of training based on how tired you get is that fatigue is not the means by which we develop greater strength or power. We develop strength and power by exposing our bodies to greater and greater demands for these qualities over a long period of time. If we don't give ourselves the time and if we don't create regular and progressive overloads, improvements will only happen by chance.

Program design, then, is the method by which you attempt to get the right amount of overload at the appropriate intervals for improvement. It is also where you learn the discipline to go heavy sometimes, light at other times, and look for progress in your numbers rather than in how sore you become.

PRINCIPLES OF TRAINING

There are many ways to get better or stronger for sport. For every world-class performance, there is a different method of getting in top shape. The method you use is not important as long as that method embraces some simple principles of training. The principles that make up good training are as follows:

SPECIFICITY

Your training should involve movements, durations, and intensities similar to your sport. We see specificity in two distinct realms:

- **METABOLIC SPECIFICITY:** Training should load energy systems similar to your sport and the training should be done in regard to the durations used in performance.

- **MOTOR SPECIFICITY:** Training should enhance the foundations of movement in the sport. This does not mean that training should simulate climbing, only that it should be done in a way that can be applied to the effort. This can include partial movements (such as campusing) and static holds (such as hangboards).

Training can be either motor or metabolically specific in a given session, and occasionally it will be both. Generally, these values are trained together more frequently as we get closer to times we want to climb well.

OVERLOAD

"WHAT GOT YOU HERE WON'T GET YOU THERE."

If you're going to get better, you've got to overload your body more than you did to get to this level. This means more load, longer sets, more days on, etc...depending on your training goals. This is perhaps the hardest of the principles to push - what we did last time seemed so hard! The progress between grades and between weights in the gym and between edge sizes on the hangboard comes slower and slower each time around, but it's the overload - trying against something that seems near-impossible at first - that keeps us progressing.

It is also a principle that is easily overdone in the short-term and underdone in the long-term. We tend to try to push too fast in a short period, suffer from over reaching / over training, and stay in a bad cycle. Athletes tend to think that if they can just go hard enough in this session, they'll somehow break through faster.

We'll talk again and again about taking the long view on strength in this book. Once you find that fine line between patience and drive you'll be on the road forward.

PROGRESSION

Progression is similar to overload, but is a more encompassing principle. Yes, we need to increase the load on the athlete over the course of a cycle and over the course of a career, but we also need that athlete to progress the complexity of training, and the demand on the energy-supplying systems of the body. This means progressing from relatively easy movements on the climbing wall such as high steps and crimps to more difficult patterns like compression moves or drop-knees. It can mean progressing from simple exercises like the deadlift to the kettlebell swing, to the kettlebell snatch.

Progression also means taking what was once a strength exercise, something that was very near a maximal effort, and making it something that you can do repeatedly. Perhaps you could do just one pull-up as a novice climber. Eventually you got to two, then three, and so on. At first, the progress is a function of improved strength, but once you get to about 5 or more you're really seeing progression in your body's ability to endure a high load. Continuing to attack progression is a clear path to improvement.

VARIABILITY

In climbing, you'll never do the exact same move on two different climbs. Unlike a sport where you perfect a hard skill such as pole vaulting or running, climbing requires you to have a much broader set of soft skills that can apply across a variety of types or movements, holds, and angles. In training, we tend to work just one pattern of a movement, such as a two-hand pull-up with the arms at shoulder width, or a straight-backed standard deadlift.

Variability in training, including occasionally changing the holds you use on the hangboard, the exercises you select in the weight room, the schedule you train, whether you use one limb at a time or two, and so on, is a key to continual progress.

Variability does not mean randomness. Each of your variations of exercise should go through a full cycle of several sessions of overload and progression before being changed. If you don't repeat an exercise long enough to see positive progress, it can be argued that it is of negligible value.

MASTERY

In a skill-based sport such as climbing, there are almost infinite varieties to the movements we learn. At each step, these movements get more difficult to improve, the curve becoming ever-flatter as you progress.

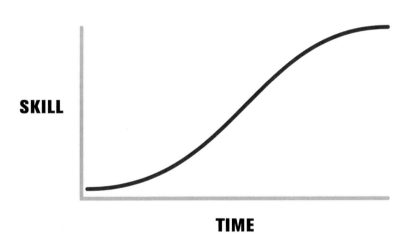

SKILL

TIME

Mastery is the continual pursuit of these ever-more difficult skill steps. The enemy of mastery is impatience. Many of us feel entitled to the next grade, we feel all the work we've put in deserves a bigger payout. When you get close to your limits, though, progress is slower and more difficult than you ever might have imagined.

Mastery is the willingness to come back to even basic movements with a mind toward improving them. Climbers tend

to start with very few skills that get them up the rock. After a few months or years of practice, they get pretty good at the basic skill sets for good movement. The mistake is that we get "good enough" and then stop trying to get the movement perfect. The majority of climbers that have plateaued in the mid-grades are likely victims of this error - their movement is OK, and so they fall into looking at getting stronger fingers and more endurance as their only way forward.

Mastery of movement allows you to progress even with modest levels of strength and power. Mastery should be the core of all your training.

SIMPLICITY

"EVERYTHING SHOULD BE MADE AS SIMPLE AS POSSIBLE, BUT NOT SIMPLER."

People who tend to enjoy programming tend to complicate it unnecessarily. Complicated methods of periodization, of load cycling, of super-overloads, drop sets, partials, and others should be tools reserved for elites who have exhausted all other possible avenues to improvement. Most of us can get more out of sleeping better and backing off on the beer than we can from complicated programming.

On the flip-side, a program that consists of just one or two exercises repeated for months on end might be too simple to help us progress. An example is the bouldering-with-friends-on-every-tuesday-and-thursday-forever program. Fun, simple, and probably only good to get you to 70% of your potential.

When you're stuck, it's a good practice to look at how many variables you are trying to control. It's good to look at how many things you are trying to improve. The most successful plans focus on improving just one or two simple facets of your fitness at once. Keep it manageable, flexible, and easy to explain - if you can't explain your training in two sentences, maybe it's time to rework it.

EFFORT

How hard do you try? How bad do you want it?

Every day there are athletes that put up good numbers in the gym, that absolutely crush it in preparation, but they don't put it together when it counts. Effort is the bridge between preparation and performance. If you can't muster this ability, you will never reach full potential. It is easy to argue that the climbers who progress the most consistently and quickly are those that can really try when it counts.

There are several facets to effort, but the big key is truly believing that what you say you want is what you really want. Do you want badly to send hard climbs or do you value just spending time out at the crag more? Do you like climbing the same comfortable routes every time you go to the crag, or do you want to continue to broaden your skill set? Would you rather have each move carefully dialled in before trying to redpoint, or are you willing to fight for some moves you don't quite have 100%?

Successful programs are ones that produce the desired result. Each program should be built on top of a regular climbing practice, a foundation of good strength and power, and should follow closely the principles outlined above. Your specific program matters less than the underlying principles behind its design. Remember that if your program does fail, it's probably not the hangboard protocol you did, but whether that protocol followed correct principles.

UNDERSTANDING NOTATION

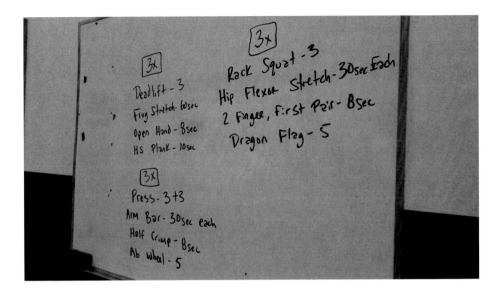

Over the past few years, a large portion of the questions we get about our books have to do with simple notation. The error is on our end - assuming someone understands how to read a workout or a plan is the worst first mistake. If they can't even read the thing, how can we expect them to do it?

This notation is important. It is something that is easy to understand once you have the hang of it, and it opens up a valuable communication channel for athletes and coaches once both are on the same page. What follows are the most common terms, phrases, and notations you'll see in our training plans and articles. These terms are used consistently in our work and although you may see some variation from other coaches or cultures, with a good grasp of the basics you should be able to figure things out soon enough.

EXERCISES

This might seem obvious, but an exercise is a specific pattern of movements designed to overload the athlete in a way that improves her function either as a human or as an athlete. Exercises are grouped together to form training sessions. Examples of exercises might be a squat, an edge hang, or a campus ladder.

SESSIONS

Sessions are groups of exercises. Also called workouts, sessions are primarily aimed at overloading a specific kind of fitness such as strength or endurance. Sessions are ideally grouped into a series that would then form a Training Plan.

TRAINING PLANS

These are groups of sessions aimed at eliciting a specific response from an athlete. This is a fundamental building block of progression, but is sometimes ignored, even by very good athletes. A training plan is generally 4-6 weeks in length and will focus on improving only one or two fitness qualities at a time.

PROGRAMS

Programs are groups of training plans. Most programs are 6 months to 5 years in length, and are build around long-term performance goals. Programs are normally quite detailed in the near-future and become less-so the further we look down the road.

SETS

These are individual cycles of exercises within a session. Most exercises are repeated several times in a session. For example, you might do 3 sets of squats and 3 sets of pull-ups in a given session. This means you would visit each exercise 3 different times in one session. Sets are divided into reps, which are the individual performances of the exercise.

REPS (OR REPETITIONS)

Reps are the number of times you perform an exercise in a given set. A session might call for 3 sets of 10 repetitions of a pull-up. This would mean you'll perform 10 pull-ups, then rest until recovered enough to do pull-ups again, do 10 more, rest, and then do 10 more. Static exercises such as planks or edge hangs on a board are usually noted in seconds, with each second held counting as one "rep." If you are training limbs individually such as in a lunge or single-arm hang, reps are generally noted in terms of # + #, such as 8+8...which means 8 reps per limb.

If the positions are held for time, reps will be noted by adding "s" or "sec" after the number. A hangboard position done for three sets of 10 seconds per hang would be noted as 3 x 10sec.

CIRCUITS

These are groups of several different exercises done in sequence. In a circuit, you perform one set of an exercise before moving on to the next exercise. Once you have completed one set of each exercise, you start the circuit again. Sessions that feature circuits will usually call for 3-8 circuits of 5-10 exercises. These are typically more endurance/conditioning-based sessions.

SUPERSETS

Supersets are two exercises done in an alternating fashion. In many of our programs, we'll superset a leg exercise and an upper body exercise, with the goal being a shorter, more efficient session. While exercising the legs, the upper body gets some degree of rest, and vice-versa. In a session, this might be noted as:

3 SETS		**3X**
5 deadlift	**OR**	A1: 5 deadlift
5 bench press		A2: 5 bench press

The A1, A2, etc. notation is indicative of the training group (A, B, C), and the exercise sequence (1,2,3).

TRI-SETS (OR "GIANT SETS")

Tri-Sets are groups of three exercise performed in series. This can be seen as a "mini-circuit." In tri-sets, it is best to alternate movement patterns, such as doing a tri-set of upper body, core, and lower body. This is an efficient way to train in the weight room or on the hangboard. Our Integrated Strength sessions are based on this model, and usually follow the hangboard/weight exercise/ mobility exercise model. If you need a testosterone boost, you can also call these "giant sets."

A tri-set might be noted as:

A1: 5 pull-ups
A2: 10 Front Squat
A3: 5 Ab Wheel

3X3 OR 4X5, ETC.

A "number x number" notation is indicative of sets x reps. If an exercise calls for 3x5 you should plan on doing three sets of five reps. Recall that an exercise performed for reps on each side is indicated by the plus (+) sign, so you might see 3 x 8+8 to indicate 3 sets of 8 reps on each side. Reps might also be noted on a set-by-set basis. In this case, you might see 5-3-2 in your session plan, indicating that the first set should be done for 5 reps, the second for 3, and the last for 2. This is usually followed by an explanation of loading parameters.

RM

RM stands for "repetition maximum." This value is useful in determining the intensity of loading in weight training. For example, your program might call for 3 sets of 3 at 85% of 1RM. In order to effectively use this information, you will need to calculate your 1-rep max for a given movement, then take the percentages. We also use variations on this idea. %MVIC, or the percentage of maximum voluntary isometric contraction, is used in calculating holds of static positions. This would be noted as a percentage of

what you could hold for a given amount of time at a given load. "Sec max" is also used. This number, such as "10 sec max" is used in prescribing static holds, usually on the hangboard.

#:#, SUCH AS 7:13

This notation is used to describe timed intervals. Simply put, the first number is the work duration and the second is the rest duration. 6 x 7:13 would mean 6 sets of 7 seconds work followed by 13 seconds rest. If the rest is not passive - sitting on the floor or walking around the gym - it is usually noted. For example, in a Rhythm Interval, you have an active rest. The sessions are usually noted as follows: 4 x 30:30, but in the session's description you are instructed to move up and down the board for 30 seconds then rest on a big jug for 30 seconds.

ROUNDS (OR SERIES)

This is an indication of how many times you would complete a circuit or group of exercises. To use the Rhythm Interval example, you may be instructed to do 3 rounds of 4 x 30:30 with 4 minutes' rest between. With this information, it is easy to figure out just how long your training should take, in the example above, you'd do 4 minutes of intervals in set 1, rest 4 minutes, do 4 minutes of intervals in set 2, rest 4 minutes, and do a final set of 4 minutes...20 minutes total.

TECHNICAL FAILURE

The era of bodybuilding ushered in the idea of training to absolute failure. This was relatively safe to do in bodybuilding workouts as the exercises were highly isolated - curls, calf raises, leg extensions and the like. You keep trying to move a load with worse and worse form in search of the elusive "pump." In the early 2000s high-intensity timed circuits became popular and with the advent of CrossFit so did including compound lifts in these circuits. Training to failure was encouraged and many injuries and serious medical issues were the result.

We encourage athletes who are trying to develop strength or power or skills to train only to the point of technical failure, the point at which you can no longer do the movement with the same quality or speed as you could at the beginning of the set. There is little value in going past this point except in the pursuit of hypertrophy (bulking up). Since hypertrophy is rarely our goal, we rarely go there.

CHAPTER 5

FOUNDATION STRENGTH:
WHAT YOU DO ALL THE TIME

PHOTO: NATE LILES

> **"**
>
> IF YOU HAVEN'T BUILT THE FOUNDATION, DON'T PAINT THE CEILING."
>
> **DAN JOHN**

When people train, they generally fall into two categories:

- The ones who get in shape a month or two before "the season."
- The ones who "train" all the time at about the same intensity.

It's likely the most effective program is in some sweet spot between. We are learning that there are certain things that every climber should do year-round, no matter the season. A basic level of athleticism is key. On top of that, it is important to assess the needs of upcoming trips and goal routes, and ramp up to them during certain parts of the year.

Avoiding dropping too far away from your highest levels of fitness makes those levels all the easier to re-attain. As W.C. Heinz wrote in his classic boxing novel, The Professional:

> *"He looks in perfect shape."*
> *"He's never been far off in seven years," Doc said. "When you come to the last step it shouldn't be any steeper than the rest."*

Foundation is the hard-earned strength you don't want to pay for twice. Getting strong is a real chore and can take years and years. Staying strong, well, that's the key to being able to do all the specific stuff. If you don't have to worry about strength, conditioning is a snap.

Foundation strength is what you do every week. It is not forced, it is coaxed. It is the kind of strength that you can't fake, and it's the kind you want to prioritize in every phase of your training.

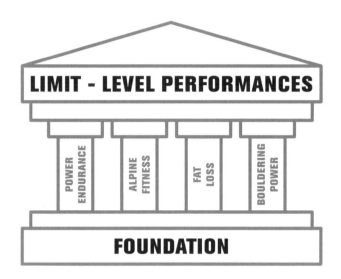

Improvement in conditioning is limited, each facet being dependent on a strong foundation. The bigger the foundation, the better your conditioning.

WHY STRENGTH AS A FOUNDATION AND NOT POWER OR ENDURANCE?

Strength is the basis for all the facets of fitness. Power is strength displayed explosively, and is fully dependent on how strong you are. Endurance is your strength (or power) displayed over time. Strength is what is called a "persistent" factor of fitness, meaning it is slow to build, but tends to stay around once you build it.

Having the ability to stand from a squatting position, to maintain an erect posture, to pull your body up to an overhead bar, or to maintain torso stiffness sets the basis for being able to do all of those things faster or for greater durations. The easier a movement is for your body, the more you can repeat that movement.

Although explosiveness is the basis of movement in our sport, it is dangerous without the strength to keep the body intact. Without the ability to create massive amounts of tension, our efficiency in explosive movement suffers. The same idea goes for endurance - if you are maintaining or building a base by doing lots of easy pitches, you are going to have a very hard time when the moves get hard. Without a high level of strength in the fingers, you're going to risk injury and you're going to be working at a high percentage of your max strength when you really shouldn't be.

WHAT DOES FOUNDATION STRENGTH LOOK LIKE?

"

ABSOLUTE STRENGTH IS THE GLASS. EVERYTHING ELSE IS THE
LIQUID INSIDE THE GLASS. THE BIGGER THE GLASS, THE MORE OF
'EVERYTHING ELSE' YOU CAN DO."

BRETT JONES

Think about it like you're building a house: the deeper you pour the concrete footings, the wider the slab, and the thicker the sub-floor, the bigger you can build the house. You can add a garage, a second floor, an addition. Fitness is the same way - the more force you can apply and the more strain your connective tissue can take, the further you'll go in any sport. In order to build elite-level athletes, smart coaches have broken strength training down to *movement patterns*. This is simply looking at fundamental human movements and designing ways to overload those patterns in the gym.

We used to train muscles, cruising the machines in the gym to wear out the pecs, the biceps, the delts, etc. until we tired out all the "parts." The problem was that just tiring out a muscle doesn't make it function correctly in a real-world setting, nor does it necessarily make it stronger. By letting muscles work together in natural movement patterns and by doing ground-based exercises, we better mimic what happens in sport. In climbing training, we address five standard movements plus finger strength - a factor that is fundamental to climbing but almost unnecessary in most other activities.

Foundation strength for climbing consists of the ability to apply high levels of force in six different ways:

1. **SQUATTING:** Climbers should have the ability to stand from a sub-parallel (butt very close to the ground) squat position with an additional load somewhere near bodyweight. Alternatively, they would display the ability to do a single-leg squat with either leg from the same position at bodyweight or a little more.

2. **HINGING:** The "posterior chain" of muscles are responsible for keeping our bodies upright and, in climbing, our hips against the wall, even in roofs. The hip hinge exercises are likely the biggest bang for your buck in general strength. Most people should be able to deadlift around 1.5 to 2x bodyweight, and hold the Sorenson Test for 2 minutes. (The Sorenson Test is simply done by holding a face-down plank on a glute ham machine for time.)

3. PRESSING: We downplay the need for pressing strength in climbing, but strong pressing muscles - the ones we use to push loads away from the body in training - are fundamental to good movement, joint stability, and continued progress in our pulling strength. A foundation level of strength for women would be a ⅔ bodyweight bench press or a 1/4 bodyweight single arm overhead press. For males, a bodyweight bench press is a good number, and an overhead single arm press between ⅓ and ½ bodyweight is great.

4. PULLING: We all pull as an adjunct to our climbing, yet most of us already have much more than enough strength in this movement. The rowing motion is more useful to train than the pull-up, and our standards reflect this. Female climbers should be able to do a strict dumbbell row at half bodyweight, and complete 5 tactical pull-ups. Male climbers should be able to row ⅔ bodyweight, and complete 8 pull-ups.

5. MIDSECTION STRENGTH: We won't confuse midsection strength with having a six-pack or being able to hold a plank for 3 minutes. We look only at performance and the ability to maintain tension. Our standards for good midsection strength are 6 knees-to-elbows with no breaking tension (i.e. swinging) and the ability to do a front lever.

6. FINGER STRENGTH: There are many ways to test grip strength. Our favorite tests are to hang a 5 second max on a 20mm edge with each arm individually, and to score bodyweight for each hand on a dynamometer. More than any other factor we test, this is a highly individual measure. More important is to test regularly and look for improvements over each cycle of training.

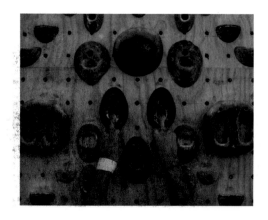

HOW OFTEN DO YOU DO IT?

"

I DON'T WANT ANY MESSAGES SAYING 'I'M HOLDING MY POSITION.' WE'RE NOT HOLDING A GODDAMNED THING. WE'RE ADVANCING CONSTANTLY AND WE'RE NOT INTERESTED IN HOLDING ANYTHING EXCEPT THE ENEMY'S BALLS. WE'RE GOING TO HOLD HIM BY HIS BALLS AND WE'RE GOING TO KICK HIM IN THE ASS; TWIST HIS BALLS AND KICK THE LIVING SHIT OUT OF HIM ALL THE TIME. OUR PLAN OF OPERATION IS TO ADVANCE AND KEEP ON ADVANCING. WE'RE GOING TO GO THROUGH THE ENEMY LIKE SHIT THROUGH A TINHORN."

GENERAL GEORGE S. PATTON

We train foundation strength all the time. One of the biggest mistakes you can make as an athlete is to build strength in the off season, and then let it dissipate through your performance seasons. Strength is so easy to maintain and is so useful, that it is worse than foolish not to keep it.

We recommend looking at your strength in two separate phases, either building quickly or building it slowly in a "maintenance" phase. The build up phase needs to occur just once or twice a year for 4-8 weeks, and maintenance of strength happens the rest of the time. In a standard year of thirteen 4-week cycles, count on 3 of them to be strength builds, 9 to be maintenance phases, and one to be dedicated to rest, vacation, illness, etc.

1	2	3	4	5	6	7	8	9	10	11	12	13
B	M	M	M	B	M	M	M	M	B	M	M	R

B: BUILD   **M:** MAINTAIN   **R:** RECOVER

In the build phase, most athletes will train strength 4-5 days per week, and usually integrate resistance exercise and hangboarding/grip training. We still climb during this phase, but the mindset shifts from trying to perform on the rock to trying to get stronger.

	BUILD PHASE	MAINTENANCE PHASE
SESSIONS PER WEEK	4 - 5	1 - 2
EXERCISES PER SESSION	4 - 7	3 - 5
SETS PER EXERCISE	3 - 5	2 - 3
APPROXIMATE SESSION DURATION	60 min.	30 min.

The maintenance phases normally feature low-volume sessions done in combination with climbing or specific training days. Your maintenance sessions should be such that you could climb hard the same day - no tapping out in the gym. Even in a maintenance phase, you can still see increases in your strength in some exercises.

CONSISTENCY WINS EVERY TIME

Too often, climbers get in the mindset of "getting in shape." No matter how hard you go in an on-again-off-again program, it will never measure up to a simple punch-the-clock program. Chris Sommer, Olympic coach and creator of the *Gymnastic Bodies* program, put it best when he said, "There is no amount of work you could do today that will offset the progress you could have made in a properly structured week." The same goes for a month, for a year, and a career.

When designing your training look at what you can manage on a long-term basis. Look at what you could do if you weren't feeling great, had low motivation, and were training alone. Whatever you can make yourself do on those days is really where your foundation training should start.

One of our athletes comes to the gym no matter what. Sometimes he's not feeling it and will do nothing more than a few minutes of jogging and some movement prep. Other days are fantastic. Year after year, he continues to reach his goals. The habit of showing up is the key to his long-term success.

TRAINING PLANS ARE BUILT ON A STRONG FOUNDATION

So you want to train for bouldering or alpine climbing or have a month planned at Ceuse. Everything starts with the base. Most of our programming involves planning which times of year to place a good strength cycle, and which times of year to let athletes loose to perform. The real beauty of having a good base of strength is that you can just build a specific conditioning cycle right on top of your low-volume strength training. The phases, then, are not discrete, but are "stacked."

An athlete might spend November and December building strength in the weight room and on the hangboard, then back off to 2 days per week of 20-30 minutes of strength work. They'd maintain this level for the next three months while ramping up power and maybe their anaerobic endurance before focusing completely on sending for 2 more months. In June, it would be back to a strength cycle, before heading into another low-volume strength period where the climber again develops power and conditioning before the fall redpoint season.

The key that differentiates this kind of thinking is that strengthening never stops, which is fundamental to long-term athletic success. In the following section, we'll talk about the many good ways there are to plan a year of training.

LOG. PROG. RP PREP SEASON

	SESSION 1	SESSION 2	SESSION 3	SESSION 4
1	GEN STR 1	GEN PWR 1 FINGERS	GEN END 1	GEN STR 2
	[CRAG: VOLUME 3 WEEKS]			
2	GEN POWER 2 + FINGERS	GEN END 2	GEN STR 3	GEN PWR 3 + FING.
3	GENERAL ENDURANCE 3	GEN STR 4	GEN POWER 4 + FING.	GEN END 4

CHAPTER 6

PLANNING A YEAR OF TRAINING

7	SPEC STR 5	SPEC POWER 5	ALACTIC INT 1	SP...
	[CRAG: 1x VOL 1x 2E 1x RP]			
8	SPEC POWER 6	ALACTIC INT 2	SPEC STR 7	SPEC ...
9	ALACTIC INT 3	SPEC. STR 8	SPEC POWER 8	ALACTIC INT 4
10	SPEC STR (2) 1	SPEC POWER (2) 1	AER INT 1 ALAC INT 5	SPEC STR 2(
	[CRAG: 2x RP 1x VOL 1x P]			
11	SPEC POWER (2) 2	AER INT 2 ALAC INT 6	SPEC STR (2) 3	SPEC POWER
	AER INT 7 ALACTIC INT 7	SPEC STR (2) 4	SPEC. POWER (2) 4	AER INT 4 ALACTIC INT
	SPEC STR (2) 5	SPEC POWER (2) 5	AER INT 5 GLYC. PEAK 1	SPEC STR(2
	[CRAG: RP DAYS ONLY]			
	SPEC. POWER (2) 6	AER INT 6 GLYC. PEAK 2	SPEC STR (2) 7	SPEC POW

PHOTO: STEVE BECHTEL

"

IT IS BETTER TO UNDERTRAIN THAN TO OVERTRAIN. YOU WILL STILL SUPERCOMPENSATE, BUT NOT TO THE SAME DEGREE. ONCE YOU OVERTRAIN, THE BODY WILL PLUMMET AND FIGHT TO RETAIN BALANCE. SMALLER CNS DEMANDS OVER A LONGER PERIOD OF TIME RESULT IN MORE ACCEPTANCE AND GREATER IMPROVEMENT, WHILE THE RUSH TO GET MORE DONE LEADS TO UNCERTAINTY DOWN THE ROAD."

CHARLIE FRANCIS

Getting good takes time. So does getting strong. A common mistake climbers make is to look only at the day in front of them or the coming week. A smart athlete builds a pretty good picture of his training program long before the workouts occur. If you are serious about progress, you should have at least a general idea of what you are doing a month from now, six months from now, and next year.

This need not be complicated or overly detailed. In fact, the simpler your long-term plan is, the better. To start, you should follow the simple steps below:

1. Write out a line-per-week calendar, preferably in a spreadsheet (or use a simple online version). This should have one line for each of 52 weeks, with columns for that week's date, events, and training phase. You should also add a column entitled "week of phase."

2. Place fixed events, comps, trips, holidays, etc. in the calendar, as far out as you know them.

3. Plan your desired performance times, such as weeks when conditions are particularly good, when you might have a climbing trip coming up, etc.

4. Start planning backward from these performance phases.

Example of a week-per-line calendar

WEEK #	DATE	EVENTS/TRIPS	TRAINING PHASE
1	6-JAN-2020	Bouldering Comp-Regionals	Power
2	13-JAN-2020		
3	20-JAN-2020	Travel - Home	
4	27-JAN-2020	Bouldering Comp Nationals	
5	3-FEB-2020	Vacation	
6	10-FEB-2020		Strength Maintenance
7	17-FEB-2020	Red Rocks Trip	
8	24-FEB-2020	Red Rocks Trip	Recovery
9	2-MAR-2020		
10	9-MAR-2020		Strength Build
11	16-MAR-2020		
12	23-MAR-2020		
13	30-MAR-2020		

When we say plan backward, you simply want to start training with the idea of aiming your sessions toward a desired outcome, such as bouldering, alpine climbing, or sport routes. You want your practice in the rock gym and at the crag to reflect the upcoming goal. In the weight room, we recommend training foundation strength, and varying the program only slightly as you move into a performance phase.

DO YOU NEED PERIODIZATION OR JUST VARIATION?

Periodization is a method for planning to train specific facets of fitness during strategically planned phases of the year. In general, these phases aim to peak certain facets of the athlete's fitness during key times. Although an attractive structure for planning, the effectiveness of a periodized plan is often called into question.

Many climbers jump into a periodized program for training with both feet, not understanding that such programs are advanced tactics for squeezing the last little bit of performance out of an athlete...not a first intervention. Periodized plans are difficult to implement in a climber's training, and are largely unnecessary. Instead, we suggest training facets of climbing such as strength and power at a maintenance level year-round, adding in some specific endurance work strategically throughout the year.

That being said, we do suggest that athletes vary their loading throughout the week or month. This could be as simple as climbing routes one day, boulders on the next training day, and maybe doing some easy circuits on the next. Similarly, one could train in a single mode (such as weight training) but would vary the intensity as the week progresses. This might mean doing 5 sets of 3 reps on day one, 3 sets of 5 on day 2, and perhaps 4 sets of 8 on day 3. This way we avoid overtraining one particular load or volume, and can progress more effectively.

LOGICAL PROGRESSION FOR STRENGTH

In Steve's book, Logical Progression, he suggested a 3 or 4 session sequence alternating between a strength session, a power session, and an endurance session before repeating the cycle. This "nonlinear" approach works well for maximizing performance over longer cycles - an important consideration for climbers who like to send difficult routes more that 2-3 times per year.

In the spirit of building a foundation program, we suggest that one could apply a Logical Progression-type mindset to a strength program. Instead of focusing on a wide array of facets of climbing fitness, the most functional application of nonlinear cycling in this book would be to switch between three facets of strength as you progress through your training cycle. A nonlinear approach might look like this:

DAY 1: 4 exercises, 4 sets each, high loads (90+% of max)
DAY 2: 6 exercises, 2-3 sets each, medium-high loads (70-90% of max)
DAY 3: 3 exercises, 3-4 sets each, explosive movements

These efforts should include several of the compound exercises described later in this book such as squats and presses, and would ideally be combined with some finger strength training. These are low-volume sessions and could be performed on the same day as performance climbing at the crag. An example two-week cycle might look like this:

	M	TU	W	TH	F	SA	SU
WEEK 1	High		Medium / Climb		Explosive		High / Climb
WEEK 2		Medium	Climb		Explosive / Climb		Climb

The big key with this approach would be to decide whether your focus is on performance or on gaining strength. The same cycle can be used either way, it's just that your focus shifts. If you are going to focus on getting stronger, push the loads hard, load up the hangboard exercises, and don't worry about sending hard in the gym or at the crag. It is not appropriate to stop climbing altogether, but it should be seen more as "movement practice" than performance.

Once your focus moves to doing hard climbing, you would look at trying to maintain loads in the gym, back off on total weekly sessions in strength and increase both the load and volume of the climbing. In a performance-focused phase, training even as infrequently as one out of five days should be sufficient to maintain strength through an entire cycle. A performance phase might look like this:

M	TU	W	TH	F	SA	SU
Climb Volume		Explosive/ Climb Low Volume	Climb Medium Volume		Climb High Volume	High Intensity RT
	Climb Low Volume		Climb Medium Volume Intensity RT		Climb High Volume	Climb Low Volume

It is important not to get stuck on the idea that certain sessions must be trained on specific days of the week. You have got to allow for flexibility in your scheduling. Even if your available training days are fixed, you can still adjust the training focus that day. Most of us are stuck with a more-or-less fixed amount of training time each week. The key to success is not letting the week govern your specifics...and not to try to force your body's adaptation to an arbitrary schedule.

If you decide to train on a nonlinear cycle, you can expect to see your training numbers move up more slowly than you might in a traditional program, but you'll see them progress longer. Most athletes on a cycle such as this will see a pause in progress after 8-10 full cycles (24-30 sessions), at which point an adjustment in exercises, frequency, or loading might restart progress.

4-DAY ACCUMULATION TRAINING

Strength training can be tough to fit in a climber's schedule. When we get really strong, often the only path forward is to add more volume to each session, which results in a protracted weight room commitment. We've wrestled with trying to figure out how to find a path to help our athletes get stronger without negatively affecting their ability to climb well on the weekends. We started by messing with typical strength programs and trying to change the volume around or eliminate exercises. Eventually, we got to reading back on programs and sessions of old time strongmen and some Olympic lifters. The basis of this program came from the training plans of Ed Coan, Paul Anderson, and Steve Justa.

The program is based on manipulating the standard supercompensation cycle seen in training. The typical cycle involves an overload and resultant decrease in strength for a short time while the body recovers. After this period - usually 24-36 hours, an athlete normally sees a small uptick in strength, called supercompensation. Normal training, say every other day, tends to coax strength forward through a series of these small cycles (see Figure 1).

FIGURE 1 - NORMAL SUPERCOMPENSATION CYCLE

When we use such a cycle, everything works fine. Over time, though, the supercompensation effect becomes less and less significant. To counter this, you've got to keep hammering the athlete with harder and harder work, resulting in longer cycles. These longer cycles start to interfere with our priority work, which is climbing. In order to get our athletes stronger and have them climb well, we built a four-day strength accumulation cycle. In this cycle, we train the athlete before he has sufficiently recovered, slowly "burying" him over 4 days. He then has 3 days away from hard training to recover (see figure 2).

FIGURE 2 - 4 DAY ACCUMULATION

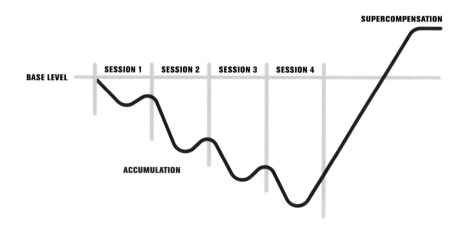

In simple terms, you will train with weights 4 days straight (Monday through Thursday), rest one day, and then climb on the weekend. You can also train in the rock gym, doing normal bouldering sessions. Follow this cycle for 4 weeks, followed by an unload week where there will be no weight training, and then repeat another 4 weeks of training with different exercises (see below). Looking at it on paper, it seems like it would be too much. It isn't. In fact, the results will be surprising - especially if you are an experienced lifter.

The biggest time commitment in these sessions is actually the warm-up. Once you get into the meat of the training, you're looking at no more than 30 minutes per day.

The warm-up should consist of a normal movement preparation sequence (our typical recommendation is eight movements and takes about 6 minutes) followed by 2-3 sets of core exercises. This is followed by a few sets of Goblet Squats, Push-Ups, and Windmills (sticking to 4-6 reps each).

The main sessions are as follows (SETS x REPS):

	DAY 1	DAY 2	DAY 3	DAY 4
Upper Body Press	3x3	4x5		2x8
Squat / Quad		3x3	4x5	2x8
Upper Body Pull	4x5		3x3	2x8
Hip Hinge	2x3	2x3	2x3	

For the entire 4 week cycle, we use the same exercise every day for each movement pattern - boring, but effective. As you can see, you'll get a heavy day of 3 sets of 3, a higher volume day of 4 sets of 5, and a lighter volume, lighter load day on the 4th day. Each set should be done with loads that match the reps - you should be able to finish each rep, but it shouldn't be easy. Never go to failure. If you hit all the reps without much problem, go up in weight on the next session.

PHOTO: MATT ENLOW

Select your exercises from the following:

UPPER BODY PRESS: Bench Press, Push Press, or 1-Arm Kettlebell Press.

SQUAT / QUAD: Rack Squats, Walking Lunges, or Front Squats

UPPER BODY PULL: Pull-Ups, Pull-Downs, or Dumbbell Rows

HIP HINGE: Deadlift or Sumo Deadlift (we keep the sets and reps low on these because of the tremendous total-body involvement. Too much work here slows our recovery.)

As we said above, you'll stick to the same four exercises for the entire four weeks, then can switch exercises in the following phase. For example:

PHASE 1: Bench Press, Rack Squat, Dumbbell Rows, Deadlift

PHASE 2: 1-Arm KB Press, Walking Lunges, Pull-Ups, Sumo Deadlift

Above all, follow through to the end of this cycle. Be conservative with your progressions; you don't need to be adding weight every week. Also, keep in mind that strength is a long-term commitment. If you could add real strength in just a week or two, we'd all be strong!

WAVES OF CHANGE

When do we go harder and when do we back off? How frequently should we change training programs? In the real world, we see examples of athletes seeing good results on a wide variety of different plans. Highly structured and detailed plans work for some, and going by feel works for others. In fact, just about any plan will work if it follows the basic principles of training listed earlier.

The one plan that tends to stop athletes dead in their tracks after just a short time is one where each week is structured exactly the same and there is no variation except a slow progression of load. If you tend toward this type of training - even if it is as simple as always bouldering Wednesdays and climbing outside on the weekends - you need to look at cycling the volume of your training.

At the very least, you should aim for two facets of variation in your training cycle.

1. A yearly variation that allows for two periods of 3-4 weeks reduced volume, perhaps in December and July. If you are always able to train at the same level, it is simply an indication that you're not going hard ever.

2. A weekly variation that features one very intense session and one very easy session every single week.

These simple interventions are the most basic and functional of training changes, but also produce the best results.

CHAPTER 7
RECOVERY TRAINING AND DELOADING

PHOTO: MEI RATZ

There is a yin-yang relationship between training and recovery. We push our bodies to adapt to greater stress, and the body reacts by getting better at handling the stress. We quite literally break ourselves down through training, and the body gets stronger while it recovers. In the pursuit of higher and higher levels of performance, some athletes try to upset this balance. We mistakenly think that adding just a little more weight or a few more laps or a couple more seconds hanging will give us that needed boost to reach the next level. As admirable as it seems, no additional loading can help if you don't also allow for additional rest.

In this chapter we'll discuss two important factors in training: recovery and deloading. Recovery training is all about maximizing your rest and recuperation on a weekly or daily basis. It's the stuff you'll have to create daily habits around, and it will be your secret weapon when it comes to really reaching beyond your current limits. Deloading happens on a larger scale, and deals with taking large chunks of time away from hard training in order to recuperate from heavy training stresses and peak performances.

RECOVERY TRAINING

We get good at pushing hard into training. We all have been in that super-pumped zone or so sore we can barely move the next day, or so exhausted from a week's training that we stay on the couch the whole weekend. As good as learning to go hard is, there is a critical time of "going easy" that can make all the difference in training.

For most of us, the opposite of training hard is simply not training. Taking it easy in the afternoon or having a couple of rest days or sleeping in on Saturday is about all there is to it. When you're young, this might be all you need. But as we age or start to train harder, we have got to turn up the recovery dial.

You'll often hear coaches caution against not going so hard and to recommend reducing volume or intensity to maximize gains. This isn't bad advice, but we just don't see avid climbers willing to do that. Since we know you are going to be hard to convince to do less training, what we want you to do is get serious about recovering. In fact, we insist that our athletes think of *recovery training* instead of rest. Once you're as serious about recovering as you are about training, you'll see gains you can't believe.

Recovery is a major growth area in sport science. Understanding that we can actually improve athletes quality and speed of recovery has led to some really good practices over the past couple of decades. From better tissue care, to better fueling, to better session design, there are many ways to recover better so you can train better. Below, we outline the eight strategies that we've seen the most successful and easy to implement. We have only included strategies that are workable in the real-world with a normal person's budget.

SLEEP MORE.

Most of us have a habitual sleep pattern, and will go to bed roughly the same time each night. At the other end, we wake to an alarm and race into the day. Although there are still many unanswered questions in the realm of sleep's relationship to exercise performance, it's been shown over and over that deprivation of sleep is damaging to motor coordination and sport performance.

Some studies suggest that adding as little as 15 minutes more sleep per day can enhance recovery by nearly 5%.

We do know that sleep enhances protein synthesis and boosts immune function, so there are many reasons to help yourself to more. It's hard to add sleep in the morning - most of us leave just enough time to race through our routines and get out the door. The best tactic is to get into bed just 15 minutes earlier. Believe it or not, climbing a grade harder might be more important than watching the last season of Narcos.

EAT AFTER TRAINING.

You've heard the hype - "Eat a 4:1 ratio of carbohydrate to protein within 40 minutes of a training session, ideally in the form of X brand recovery drink." Although simple enough, it's hard to justify trying to get an exact ratio of macronutrients in a specific time window when you don't really need to. The more research into recovery nutrition they do, the more flexible these guidelines get. The current wisdom is simply to eat within a couple of hours after a session, and to make sure that you have a full serving of protein at that time. Although a recovery drink or a glass of chocolate milk are possible choices, a sandwich, a salad with steak or chicken, or even an omelet would be fine, too. Aim for 150-250 calories, unless your training falls right before mealtime, in which case a normal meal would be appropriate. Things to avoid would be alcohol in excess or a purely carbohydrate snack.

DRINK MORE WATER.

Don't be one of those obsessive hydration people who buy into the idea that somehow we're always dehydrated. The thirst response, it turns out, is a good indicator of whether you are low on fluids or not. That being said, many athletes drink very little actual water. Coffee drinks, energy drinks, soft drinks, and alcohol make up a large percentage of a typical person's intake. Although all of these drinks help us to stay hydrated to some degree, water tends to absorb better and is markedly less expensive.

We're sold the idea of electrolyte energy or recovery drinks so often that we take the idea as gospel. There are many studies that support carbohydrate intake during endurance activity. Our concern is not improved cardiovascular performance, however. We just need liquid.

It turns out that being under-hydrated can prolong soreness and extend recovery times. The easy solution is to drink a bit more during sessions than you normally do, and then to drink 20+ ounces of water after a session. This ties in well with your recovery meal above. A sandwich and a glass of water after training will provide a good base for being able to train hard again tomorrow.

TAKE A NAP.

The benefit of short naps during the day is huge, especially when it comes to recovery from exercise. More sleep at night is good, but naps are great. The major benefit of napping is an increase in anabolic hormonal activity, but getting you out of the "Go-Go-Go" cycle is probably good, too. A nap can increase release of hormones, increase protein synthesis, and improve cognitive function. Optimal napping for athletes occurs within 2 hours of your main training for the day, 3 or more hours before normal bed time, and should only be 15-25 minutes in duration - longer naps can negatively affect nighttime sleep.

DO YOUR CARDIO.

OK, this sounds crazy coming from two guys who continually argue against nonspecific training for climbing performance, but bear with us. When we look at recovery, one of the big keys is movement of "bad stuff" out of the muscles and movement of "good stuff" into them. One simple way to accelerate this process is to elevate the heart rate and body temperature slightly.

It's important that you look at heading out the door for these sessions as recovery rather than as a chance to burn a few calories or improve your endurance. As a general rule, you should look at

PHOTO: NATE LILES

doing 30-60 minutes of easy activity - such as hiking, easy cycling, or easy running - most days of the week. You should keep your heart rate below 60% of your maximum at all times, and most of your time should be spent well below even this mark.

TAKE A COLD SHOWER.

This one sucks, but it is surprisingly effective, especially if your muscles are sore. Cold baths or showers (10+ minutes in duration) have been shown to improve strength and power recovery times, and should be part of your arsenal of recovery modes after especially intense training.

You can also explore contrast showers or baths. In this recovery mode, you'd spend 2-3 minutes under the coldest water you can stand, followed by the same duration under the hottest you can stand. Repeating this cycle 2-3 times in a session, and ending with cold has been shown to have a greater effect on reducing soreness than cold alone. Some research suggests that it can help improve recovery times, but it doesn't seem as effective as cold alone.

BACK OFF ON THE BEER.

Although kicking back a few beers at the end of a climbing day can be seen as an integral part of our culture, it's probably not the best way for an athlete to recover. As much as we want our alcohol to be a good thing, research shows that consuming more than a couple of drinks will increase the time it takes you to recover from training. The good news is that one or two beers or glasses of wine seem to have no ill-effect on recovery. Good news if you can stop there. This one goes hand-in-hand with trying to drink more water. Before you hit the bar, drink a full glass of water...you'll save money and climb better the next day.

EAT PROTEIN BEFORE (OR DURING) TRAINING.

There is some benefit to consuming small amounts of protein before or during training to jumpstart the recovery process even before you've beaten yourself down. Researchers suggest consuming small portions (so as not to upset the digestion) slightly before or during strength and power exercise sessions. Because protein digests slowly, you can only do so much...try starting with around 30-50 calories in the form of a small snack or protein drink, and work your way up from there.

Recovering from training is easy at first, but as you advance in what you can load yourself with, you should be advancing how you deal with it. This is not an exhaustive list, and the suggestions here are merely starting points. The point we want to drive home is that there is more to getting better than going hard. If you put some focus into what happens after training, you will get more out of each session, and it might be the secret sauce you've been looking for to gain that next grade.

RECOVERY POINTS

In 2016 and 2017, we helped develop a recovery program for national-level competitive youth climbers. The idea was to emphasize how important recovery is, and to keep them from climbing before and after practice...and every day in between. Coaches can see that performance is limited when training volumes get too high. In order to help the athletes understand recovery, we put forth a list of recovery modes and session types, and assigned each a point value. The training list looked like this:

- Bouldering, 1 hour: 10 points

- Hard Route Climbing, 1 hour: 10 points

- Weight Training, 1 hour: 10 points

- Easy Climbing (@ OS level or below), 1 hour: 5 points

- Speed Training, 1 hour: 10 points

- Other sport activities, 5-10 points per hour determined by intensity

The athletes were simply guided to add up as many recovery points as they had "spent" in training before they could climb or train again. The recovery points were as follows:

- Sleep, hours before midnight: 3 points per hour

- Post-training meal, at least 200 calories within an hour of session: 2 points

- Drink water (WATER ONLY!): 1 point per liter

- Napping: 5 points per nap

- Walking or easy cycling, 30-60 minutes maximum per day: 2 points

- Cold Shower (5-10 minutes): 2 points

- Hit protein goal (usually 1.5-2g/kg bodyweight): 3 points

- Foam roll or stretching (15 minutes): 1 point

So, say an athlete bouldered hard for 2 hours. The climber would then need to get 20 recovery points before they could do the next session. So, we can:

- Go to bed at 9 (9)

- Eat post-training (2)

- Take a walk (2)

- Take a cold shower (2)

- Eat enough protein (3)

- Drink 2 liters of water (2)

A youth athlete might very well be recovered sufficiently by the next day after a two hour session. Longer sessions naturally force more rest days. These numbers can vary athlete-to-athlete, but the general principle works like crazy for keeping serious competitive youth seriously competitive.

For athletes over the age of 30, we add 50% to the point value of each training session, so a bouldering hour would be 15 points, weight training 15 points, etc. Over 45, we add another 5 to each hour of activity. Older athletes can train very hard...they just need to exploit their wisdom and patience to be sure they recover well in-between.

DELOADING

Stuck is somewhere we've all been, whether it was in a specific exercise, failing at the anchors of a project, or holding a mediocre performance plateau for years on end. We all know it when it's happening, but most of us get lost when it comes to fixing the problem. Our solutions too often come back to doing more - more of what we like, more of what didn't work last time, or more of the latest exercise we saw someone else doing at the gym last week. We too easily get sucked into changing small factors in our training, and often overlook big, and simple solutions.

One of our main jobs when it comes to consulting with climbers is to help them look for ways (besides training harder) to improve. Long years ago, we learned that it's not going to be changing an exercise or two. It almost always came down to their readiness and willingness to train at specific intensity on the proper days, and taking time to come back after a long season of pushing their bodies hard.

Almost all of us default to medium intensity in each exercise or movement on the wall. Even if there is a hard crux in a problem, we increase rest between tries or switch in more moderates between, or even shorten the session - all because our bodies are asking to stay in that mid-range of effort. We default to medium-volume weeks of training, adding an extra session to weeks that feel too light, or resting more as the fatigue of a particular week

accumulates. Weeks of medium lead to months of medium, where the training load of the whole phase becomes more or less steady - easy for the body to cope with, but not really producing performance gains.

We are almost all happier and more comfortable with a basic structure of habits and routines. It's no wonder our training falls into the same pattern. Experience shows that people are much better at maintaining a fixed weekly schedule of training than allowing large variability, which can be an Achilles' heel. We know that adaptation requires both overload and recovery, that training load has to be answered with recovery load if we are to improve fitness. Most important - if we increase training demand, we also need to increase or improve recovery.

DELOAD WEEKS

This is all a long way of saying that the number one most effective intervention in restarting a stuck program is deloading. Imagine you have a pretty steady week-to-week schedule. You climb the same nights at the gym, you get to the crag on Saturday, and you do a couple of runs on the days in between. Over time, this becomes an exercise habit, which is a good thing. But habits also have a bad side, and it's that you do the same things in the same amounts at the same difficulty every time.

The normal result of this kind of training is simply staleness - a plateau. Other possible results are injury or illness...it's almost like your body will do anything to break the "exercising but not training" cycle. Across 4 weeks, your training distribution would show 25% per week, like this:

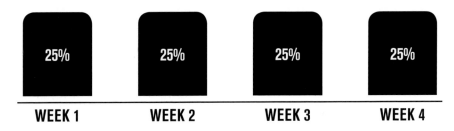

25%	25%	25%	25%
WEEK 1	**WEEK 2**	**WEEK 3**	**WEEK 4**

If you've got basic recovery mastered, as mentioned above, the easiest intervention is to move to a three-weeks-on cycle followed by a deload week at about half the volume. This is a tall order for most climbers...somehow the mindset of sticking with a schedule overpowers the strong proof that one needs recovery. "Half-volume?!" Yes. Cut back from 10 hours this week to 5 next. You might actually send harder grades again. You don't have to stick to a rigid 3-1 schedule, either...two weeks of load, then a week off, then 4 weeks of load would be fine. It's nice to schedule deloads during family vacations, times of big work commitments, or when a new season of Game of Thrones is released.

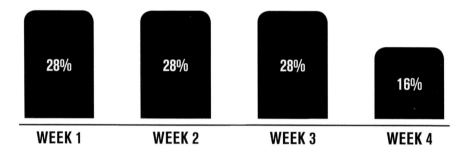

WEEK 1	WEEK 2	WEEK 3	WEEK 4
28%	28%	28%	16%

The three-weeks-on-one-week-off program works well for many people and is our first/best intervention. Some athletes start to plateau on this program, even with a good recovery week in there. If this is the case, we simply move to a progressive schedule. In such a schedule, week 1 is easy, week two is "medium", week 3 is hard, and week 4 is a recovery week. Climbers tend to scoff at such a schedule and think that they can train "hard" more than one week a month. When we talk about training hard, it's really hard. If you can go hard more often than that, you're probably mistaking *medium* for hard.

The first week should be a little easier than your normal training week. The second will feel like you're training at your normal/hard level. Week 3 should push you exceedingly hard - so much so that you're willing to really recover the following week. The training distribution (in % of one month's total training time training) should be about 22-28-35-15.

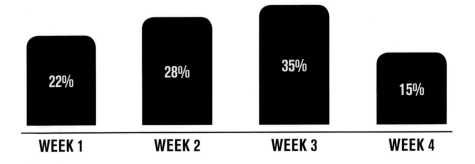

| **WEEK 1** | **WEEK 2** | **WEEK 3** | **WEEK 4** |

If you're older and tire out easily, you can still keep the same difficult training up, but you might want to stagger it a little bit. Instead of having your medium and hard weeks back-to-back, you give yourself a bit of rest every other week. The distribution on this could be 20-30-20-30, but this program tends to cause staleness fairly quickly. A better alternative is to stick with the same percentages as described in the previous paragraph, but rearrange them as 22-35-15-28 or 15-35-22-28. This distribution really forces that hard and easy week in there, and tends to produce results longer.

People sometimes have a hard time switching to this staggered style - it feels like they are "not doing enough" training on the weeks off. Well, guess what...you're not. You're recovering. In fact, only by testing your numbers can you tell if it's working. If your only way of gauging intensity is how tired you are, you are probably not maximizing your program.

LONGER DELOADING PERIODS

Athletes can go several years without a significant deload period... or at least without a formalized one. Holidays, trips, and illnesses can act as excellent respites from training without us seeing them as specific periods of recovery. Many climbers fear time off, as coming back can be physically challenging and their "feel" for the rock seems to slip away quickly. Luckily, even a 3-week period of no activity will only result in minor losses in strength and power, and most skills can be re-honed in just a week or two of concentrated effort once back on the rock.

It is our recommendation that every climber take a period of 2-3 full weeks away from climbing and hard training each year. This can be in the form of one long period of layoff, or can be three separate weeks set aside throughout the year. These cycles let your body get a "deep breath" after hard performances or trips and enhance the training sessions that follow them.

It is important to understand that an undulating level of fitness is normal. Letting yourself perform well during parts of the year and then taking some time to rebuild basic strength, focus on other parts of your life, and rebuild motivation will help assure a long and promising career.

CHAPTER 8
ADDITIONAL NOTES:
MELDING STRENGTH AND POWER
STRENGTH CREATES ENDURANCE

PHOTO: MEI RATZ

MELDING STRENGTH AND POWER

Too frequently, we try to over-categorize our training. Long-time athletes and coaches learned about training for climbing by reading about and practicing training that came from other sports. We all understood that strength and power and endurance were different entities, some of us going so far as to train all of these different qualities at different times of the year or in discrete sessions.

Although this book is focused on the need for high levels of strength and stability in climbing, we understand that strength must be paired with skill, with capacity, and with power. Power is the primary physiological need of performance rock climbing. In sports-science terms, power is simply strength displayed with

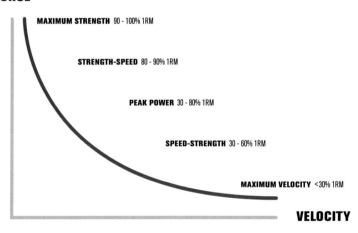

FORCE

MAXIMUM STRENGTH 90 - 100% 1RM

STRENGTH-SPEED 80 - 90% 1RM

PEAK POWER 30 - 80% 1RM

SPEED-STRENGTH 30 - 60% 1RM

MAXIMUM VELOCITY <30% 1RM

VELOCITY

a speed component, or popularly viewed as strength x speed. Power is important in sports from heavy weightlifting to baseball, with all power movements falling somewhere along the force-velocity curve.

Simply put, you can demonstrate high force with lower speed (snatching a barbell) or lower force with higher speed (throwing a baseball). Most power use by climbers ends up being somewhere in between, an a zone called "peak power."

Although power is a different animal than pure strength, both of them are used in conjunction in almost every move of a hard rock climb or boulder. We don't feel that the two should therefore be trained separately. In fact, we are much bigger fans of taking care to train them together more and more frequently as you get closer to performance phases of your training.

When designing a session that utilizes both strength and power, we keep a few key points in mind.

- Power generally should be trained fresh, so the most complex and heavy exercises in the session should be done before a lot of heavy strength. For example, box jumps should be done before heavy squat sets, and campus moves should generally be done before heavy hangboarding.

- Warm-ups should include power movements similar in velocity to the planned training.

- Warm-ups should be progressive both in terms of load and duration, i.e. start with just 1-2 reps of an exercise at 50% of working load, and slowly add both reps and weight.

- All power exercises should feature plenty of rest between. This is challenging because the sets are very short and often don't feel too hard. You should be aware of your actual performance instead of the feeling it produces - if your performance is tapering off you are either not resting enough between sets or you are simply out of juice. Don't go deep into fatigue...stop the session and plan on going hard again in a couple of days.

STRENGTH CREATES ENDURANCE

Endurance is nothing more than a display of submaximal strength carried out for a prolonged duration. In a strength-endurance sport such as climbing, pure endurance training is of limited value. Most of the sports we see as endurance sports are classified by sports scientists as cyclic aerobic activities. These sports feature movements such as pedalling or rowing or running done at very low intensity and very high volume, often to the tune of several thousand repetitions even in short workouts.

In contrast, climbing is an acyclic anaerobic activity. This means that the movements are not repetitive but feature different patterns, durations, and loads each time. The intensity is generally a bit harder than the aerobic system can handle, so much of the movement is powered anaerobically with occasional rest periods. In acyclic anaerobic sports such as climbing, wrestling, gymnastics, and martial arts, muscular endurance and strength endurance, and by default general strength, are key factors in performance.

It is well-documented that a higher level of maximum strength in a muscle or group of muscles will allow for greater levels of muscular endurance. This is partially because the muscle not having to work as hard for individual contractions, and partially due to the fact that a muscle that is not fully contracted will still allow for blood flow...which means the "bad" blood keeps pumping out of the muscle.

This is not to say that strength is the only needed facet of endurance - you'll still have to do the work of climbing up long stretches of rock - but by being stronger, climbing will take less out of you each move.

"IT IS VERY IMPORTANT THAT ALTHOUGH REPETITION OF THE SAME TRAINING...WORK OF MODERATE POWER FOR WEEKS AND MONTHS DOES NOT DELIVER A HIGH LEVEL OF SPORT RESULTS, IT SIGNIFICANTLY FORTIFIES AND STABILIZES SKILLS, CREATES A MORE PERFECT COORDINATION OF FUNCTIONS OF ORGANS AND SYSTEMS, AND STRENGTHENS THEM AND THE WHOLE ORGANISM THROUGH POSITIVE STRUCTURAL AND MORPHOLOGICAL CHANGES. THIS IS HOW THE SO-CALLED SPECIAL FOUNDATION IS BUILT."

IVIKOLAY OZOLIN

TRAINING

In this book, we divide foundation training workouts into four major sections. With each type of training there is a *warm-up* and *movement preparation* section of the training. We describe specific *finger and grip strength* exercises, and we describe *total-body strength* exercises. Finally we include *mobility and flexibility drills* to help get the most out of your newfound strength. Most of the programs described later in the book feature components from all four types of exercises.

   As with any good session, we'll start with the warm-up.

PHOTO: MATT ENLOW

CHAPTER 9
STARTING THE ENGINE:
EFFECTIVE WARM-UPS FOR STRENGTH TRAINING

Training sessions are only optimized if the athlete is ready for them.
We want to avoid injury, of course, but we also want to be sure
the muscles are ready to train at high loads. By using an effective
warm-up and movement preparation sequence, we can get more
out of each training day.

In the previous edition of this book, Steve outlined a couple
of very good movement preparation sequences that we use in
our gym. The problem was that none of the readers took this
sequence seriously, and skipped it altogether. It might have been
that the movements seemed too easy, or that the climbers felt
funny doing them while their friends did more traditional warm-
ups. Regardless, we revamped the warm-up to be more simple,
quick, and involve just one kettlebell or dumbbell.

The general warm-up includes five exercises. Start with slow,
full-range movements, and do up to ten repetitions (based on your
ability to do them well) of each exercise. The exercises are the
Push-Up, the Kettlebell Swing, the High Windmill, the Inchworm
to Shoulder Opener, and the Prying Squat. Do 2-3 rounds of this,
progressing load as you see fit.

WARM-UP EXERCISES

THE PUSH-UP

The Push-Up is a well known and easy-to-perform upper body pressing exercise. With a little practice and care, an athlete can perform it well with no fear of sore shoulders or back pain. If he is sloppy, the value of the movement can be compromised. An important consideration is that although simple, the push-up does require focus and assessment. Chances are you learned the exercise as a very young person and have been a bit sloppy with your form. Take the time to get it right and it will serve you well in the future.

To start, place the hands just slightly wider than shoulder width and hold the entire body tight - no sagging hips. You can assure this position by flexing and holding the glutes and quads tight while bracing the abs. Lower the chest toward the floor, stopping with the chest about one inch from touching. Athletes with better shoulder mobility may feel comfortable touching the chest to the floor with each rep. Hold the neck in line with the back and look straight down or forward, not at the feet and not up. Press back up to a straight-arm position at the top.

Bodyweight Push-up
Start

Bodyweight Push-up
Halfway

Bodyweight Push-up
Bottom

This exercise can be regressed by placing the hands on a bench, box, or racked barbell. Although progressions are not necessarily appropriate in the warm-up, you can obviously make the push-up harder by elevating the feet or spreading the distance between the hands.

Athletes should take a serious look at their push-up ability. If the whole body - from the heels to the head - is not moving at the same time through a full range, the movement should be regressed into an incline until this ability is achieved.

| Incline Push-up | Incline Push-up | Incline Push-up |
| Start | Halfway | Bottom |

THE SWING

The kettlebell swing is an explosive hip hinge movement. The action is to rapidly swing a kettlebell between the knees as you extend the body to a full upright position. There are a lot of joints involved in this movement, so there tends to be a big learning curve. We start the swing in a "hike" position, with the feet planted at a bit wider than shoulder width and the hands outstretched and holding the bell. For more details on this lift, see the Exercises section later in the book.

| KB Swing | KB Swing | KB Swing | KB Swing |
| Hike | Between Legs | Halfway | Finish |

The athlete loads up the heels and with a tight core, pulls the bell back and through the arch of the legs while standing up. Good cues include "thumbs to bum" or forearms on the inside of the thighs.

From the hinged position with the bell at the back position, the athlete extends the hips and stands straight up, with the quads, glutes, and abs all bracing at the top. The arms should be seem to act more as "ropes" or "chains" and should not be used to lift the bell.

Take care not to squat during the movement. The knees should bend only enough to allow the bell to pass directly through the triangle formed by the knees and hips. Take care also not to attempt to swing the bell too high. Maximum power and effectiveness in the swing is achieved when the bell reaches about chest height.

THE HIGH WINDMILL

The high windmill is a shoulder mobility and stability drill and a hip stretch all rolled into one movement. Although a bit complex to learn, this is an excellent movement for climbing and should earn a place in every climber's warm-up sequence.

| High Windmill Start | High Windmill Foot Position | High Windmill Halfway | High Windmill Bottom |

Hold a single kettlebell at full extension overhead with the left arm. We like kettlebells for this movement because the weight's center of gravity helps pull the arm back into a good stretch as you lean into the movement. With both feet facing to the right, bend at the hip (not at the low back) and slowly rotate forward and down, pushing the left hip out to the side as you descend. You will want to maintain a straight spine as you bend and twist to the side. It is easy to let the low back do the work here, and we want to avoid that.

Stop the range as soon as the hip flexibility would cause you to bend at the lower back...the low back must remain straight for the entire movement. Reverse the movement to complete the rep. Always start with your weaker side and match reps with the stronger side.

INCHWORM TO SHOULDER OPENER

This series of movements is not only a good hip mobility drill, it is an appropriate warm-up for the muscles of the torso and shoulder. It marries well with the High Windmill, and should be done slowly and in control.

Inchworm
Start

Inchworm
Hands on Ground

Inchworm
Inching Out

Inchworm
Push Up Pos.

Inchworm
Shoulder Opener
Foot to Hands

Inchworm
Shoulder Opener
Top Pos.

Inchworm
Inching In Pos. 1

Inchworm
Inching In Pos. 2

The movement starts in a standing position. Fold forward at the hip (bending the knees slightly if necessary) and place the palms of the floor. Walk the hands forward, but once you reach the "push-up" position, bring the right leg forward to rest just outside the right hand. Pick up the right hand and open toward the knee in front of you and reach upward, rotating the chest as far as possible.

Return to the push-up position, then repeat on the other side. Finish the rep by walking the feet forward to regain the start position.

THE PRYING SQUAT

One of our favorite hip mobility and squat preparation drills, this move first requires that you can get into a squat position at all! Heels should be planted, the back should be upright, and you should sit as low as possible - hips between heels. Place the elbows between the knees, press your palms together, and gently pry out on the legs forcing the knees apart. You can use a kettlebell held in the "goblet" position to help stabilize this bottom position if necessary. Relax into the position, sway the hips slightly to help them move lower into the squat. Hold the position for several seconds, before slowly returning to the start position. 3-4 repetitions of several seconds each is sufficient.

Prying Squat
Start

Prying Squat
Start

Prying Squat
Right Prying

Prying Squat
Left Prying

CHAPTER 10
FINGER AND GRIP STRENGTH

PHOTO: SAM LIGHTNER, JR.

You know it. Finger strength is where it all begins or ends in rock climbing. At some point, we all confront the fact that our fingers just can't hold onto certain holds that we'd like them to hang on. With this in mind, we all clearly understand the need to build great strength in these little digits.

From day one, we build strength in the fingers just through climbing. Not too far into our careers, most of us figure out that using a hangboard or other implements can enhance our finger strength beyond just climbing. We start to do sets and reps of edge hangs and we start to feel like little holds are just that much easier to use than before. Building finger strength, though, is different than building strength in other parts of the body. First, the strength gains come more from changes in the forearm muscles' ability to effectively recruit muscle fibers and coordinate their actions than from size gains or changes in the muscle fibers. Second, the connective tissue structure of the fingers is improved - but this takes a desperately long time. Repeat: THIS TAKES A LONG TIME!

The mistake we make is that we develop expectations of progress, and that the progress will come in equal measure to our efforts. Unfortunately, the closer we get to our potential, the more the improvement curve flattens out.

In an effort to "beat the curve" we make unrealistic judgements of our current finger strength program, and look for better and faster means to improve. Unfortunately, it's almost never the method...it's patience and principles that move us forward. A quick review of the previous section on principles of training (p. 42) will help remind you what good training looks like. Sticking with an old

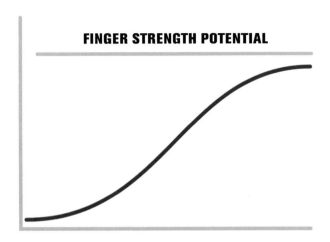

FINGER STRENGTH POTENTIAL

standby workout and keeping it simple over a 4-month period will kick you better results than any super-focused 1-month program.

This is especially true in finger strength. Having patience with the digits and keeping a mindset of using training as prevention of injuries should help. We recommend a combination of both isometric (static strength) exercises, such as edge hangs, and concentric/eccentric exercises, such as finger rolls. Although isometrics are clearly the more specific to climbing, a combination of the two types of grip strengthening will lead to greater strength gains overall and fewer injuries.

Below are descriptions of our favorite exercises for both hangboard exercises and general grip training. When to implement each will depend on the training program you choose later in the book. Don't overthink this, and don't unnecessarily complicate training until the simplest plans have been exhausted.

HANGBOARD TRAINING

Concentrated static loading on the fingers has been found to be an excellent way to make the fingers better at concentrated static loading. It might sound like a joke, but the point is that hangboard training is extremely specific to hard climbing, as we do the exact type of loading and volume we might see on the rock. Hangboard training is so specific, in fact, that many climbers have gone months away from the rock and come back to climbing with almost no decline in performance having done nothing but training on a board.

This tool is a staple of our training. Between the hangboard and loading blocks, one can simulate almost any climbing hold position. As is the usual advice in this book, a long-term view of finger strength is key, as is an understanding that going harder doesn't necessarily mean faster finger strength gains.

THE HANGBOARD EXERCISES

There are many hangboards available out there, and your gym probably has a half-dozen. Select by location, texture, and hold type, of course. You might find you need a couple of boards or even a loading block to get all the positions trained that you'd like.

As you can guess, there are dozens of possible hold position variations, as well as different elbow angles and grip widths that affect your training. In the spirit of keeping it simple, we recommend starting your hangboard practice by focusing on just five basic positions: the open hand, the half crimp, the full crimp, the pinch, and the 3-finger pocket.

OPEN HAND

In the open hand position, the second joint (PIP or proximal interphalangeal joint) is held at a level below the fingertips. This is the position recommended for holding large holds and pockets in most cases, and is quite low-stress on the finger joints.

HALF CRIMP

The half crimp is the most common hold position, and is the safest grip for most climbers. In this position, the distal phalanges are held more-or-less flat, with the PIP joint (second knuckle) kept at the same level as the fingertips. This is where we do the most training and should be the position used for max testing.

FULL CRIMP

The full crimp position is the most dangerous position we train, but it's the one climbers revert to when the chips are down on a route or boulder. We train these conservatively, and progress slowly. This grip features a closed-handed position where the second knuckle (PIP) is held above the level of the hold. A variation, the closed crimp, features a thumb rolled over the index finger's tip. This is a stronger position but can be uncomfortable for some depending on the hand's structure.

PINCH BLOCKS

The pinch grip is a fundamental hold position for many climbs, yet is difficult to train in isolation. Today's hangboards fall short of effective in training this grip position, and most of us don't have access to a good system wall on which to train pinches. For the hangboard pinch position, we have found that pinch blocks work best. These blocks, somewhere between 1.5" and 3" thick can be loaded with weight and "deadlifted" to train the pinch position. Loading blocks such as the Tension Block can also be used.

3 FINGER POCKET

The 3 finger pocket is a good basic position to train for using a variety of pocket holds. Using the index, middle, and ring fingers, you'll hang in an open-hand position, stressing the hand in the way that pocket climbing does. If you are planning a trip (or a season!) climbing on lots of pockets, consider using several 2-finger variations, as well as specific middle-finger training.

SECONDARY HOLD POSITIONS

Besides the five primary positions, we recommend using some of these secondary positions as required by your specific circumstances:

2 FINGER POCKET, FIRST PAIR   **2 FINGER POCKET, SECOND PAIR**   **2 FINGER POCKET, THIRD PAIR**

3 FINGER POCKET, OUTSIDE THREE

CONCAVE SLOPER

CONVEX SLOPER

SINGLE FINGER, INDEX FINGER

SINGLE FINGER, MIDDLE FINGER

SINGLE FINGER, RING FINGER

SINGLE FINGER, LITTLE FINGER

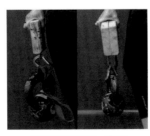

NARROW OR WIDE PINCH

VERY SMALL CRIMP (5MM TO 7MM)

GENERAL GRIP TRAINING

HEAVY FINGER ROLL

The heavy finger roll is a great movement for developing crushing strength, and is the number one exercise for building size in the forearms. This exercise is done with just a barbell, so it's a great one for almost any gym.

This exercise is best done with an Olympic bar on a power rack or squat rack to support the weight. It is important to have something (technique tray, spotting arms, or at least a bench) to catch the bar should you drop it; if you're training hard on these, you'll drop the bar occasionally. Begin with the hand held open and the bar hanging at the end of your fingertips. Slowly roll the bar up until you reach a fully closed fist with a neutral wrist, then lower it down to start position. You can perform this exercise with the bar in front of you, palms facing forward, or with the bar held behind you with palms facing back.

| Heavy Finger Roll Start (Close-Up) | Heavy Finger Roll Start | Heavy Finer Roll Halfway | Heavy Finger Roll Finish |

When starting into these rolls, begin with about half your bodyweight, and work up slowly. You can go really heavy on this one eventually, but patience is the key to avoiding injury.

GRIPPER

Hand grippers come in several different forms, most typically the coil-spring type. These are available widely, but the only ones that will really do you any good long-term are the Captains of Crush grippers from Iron Mind. These come in several different tensions, so it is possible to use progressive resistance in your training. We use these for both training crushing strength and for training isometric holding strength.

The movements are fairly obvious - hold the gripper, squeeze like crazy, and make sure the handles touch at the end of the range-of-motion. For building strength, you want to work in the realm of 10 or fewer repetitions, or an isometric hold of 10 seconds or less. If you're able to do more, the resistance is not high enough. Iron Mind makes several grippers of different levels of resistance, and we'd suggest most climbers start with the Trainer.

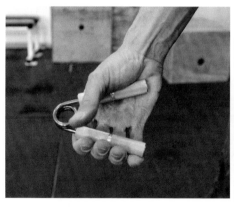

Captains of Crush Hand Gripper
Start

Captains of Crush Hand Gripper
Finish

Doing higher reps with the gripper is fine for warming-up, but it tends to fall short as an endurance training method and can be hard on the joints. Better ways to gain general forearm endurance include the hangboard, wrist curls, wrist rolls, and cable flexion/ extension workouts.

REVERSE WRIST CURLS

This is the number one exercise for developing the extensor muscles of the forearm. Although these muscles generally play a supporting role rather than being a primary mover, their development is critical to continued hand and forearm health. These are frequently a recommended exercise for rehabbing a case of lateral epicondylitis - or tennis elbow.

This exercise begins with the forearm supported by a bench or on the athlete's thigh, with the palm facing down. Holding a dumbbell or barbell, let the weight down until the wrist is completely flexed, then bring it back up to maximum extension. Move slowly here, and make sure you are keeping the handle of the dumbbell horizontal.

Reverse Wrist Curl
Flexion

Reverse Wrist Curl
Halfway

Reverse Wrist Curl
Extension

You should try to balance most of your focused flexion work with reverse wrist curls or a similar movement. Remember, though, that even the reverse wrist curl taxes your flexors - you have got to hold on to the weight while repping. Plenty of rest between sets is the key to effective training.

BAND OR PUTTY EXTENSIONS

As you might have guessed, this type of exercise works the forearm extensors. The muscle groups responsible for extension are, by design, not as strong as the flexors. Their job is stabilization and release.

We use two methods to train extension. The first is a finger "expansion" using an elastic band. To do this, simply wrap the fingers and thumb of one hand in an elastic tube or rubber band. Move from a closed position to a position as wide as you can open the band. Again, Iron Mind makes an excellent selection of tools for the job, their expansion bands come in a progressive pack of 5-6 different thicknesses. Another option is to use the rubber bands that you get when you buy asparagus or broccoli. You do buy broccoli, right?

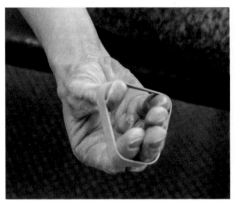

Banded Finger Extensions
Start

Banded Finger Extensions
Finish

The second method we use is with a putty, placed in a "pancake" on a table, or a tight "donut." In either case, place all the fingers and thumb in the middle of the putty and expand it slowly.

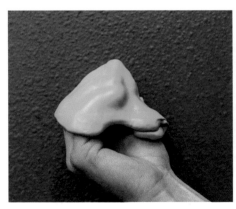

Putty Finger Extensions
Start

Putty Finger Extensions
Finish

As stated earlier, the structure of the extensors is significantly weaker and more fragile than the flexors. Avoid doing a tremendous volume of work with them at first. Most athletes can do about four times as much volume AND intensity with their flexors than extensors.

SKIN CARE AND OTHER CONSIDERATIONS

When you are training your fingers, your skin and soft tissue of the hands can take a beating. We see this most frequently on the hangboard and campus board, but it can occur in the weight room, too. Your training bag should include several items to help maximize the success of your sessions. These items include:

- Athletic tape

- Alcohol pads

- Chalk

- Nail clippers

- Nail file or sanding block

- Hold brush

- Small fan

Simple athletic tape should be available to cover nicks and cuts in the skin or to protect sensitive areas such as calluses or thin tips. We don't like the taping of painful joints for training purposes unless prescribed by a climbing-aware physical therapist or doctor.

A good, dry chalk should be used to keep the hands dry. It should also be employed to keep the boards in good shape. As a rule, you should brush the board before and after use, and never use the grips with your greasy, grubby fingers. Washing hands before and after training will keep your board clean and you healthy.

A nice brush is a big necessity. Toothbrushes are fine, but a good boar's hair brush is worth dropping some change for.

Also consider alcohol prep pads to reduce the oil on fingertips, as well as clippers and files to help keep skin smooth and reduce tearing.

Finally, if you are in a hot or humid gym, a small fan placed near the board can be a great help in keeping the fingers cool and the friction high. An inexpensive clip-on fan will fit easily in a gym bag and costs just a few dollars.

CHAPTER 11

STRENGTH TRAINING

We have argued in favor of being stronger throughout this book. If you have read this far, you probably don't need any more convincing, so we'll focus on the how. The most important thing to remember is not that you need to be stronger, it's that you need to be able to apply it. We've all seen very strong people in the gym who just couldn't execute on the rock. Clearly, lack of strength is not the issue, it's a lack of application. To make the most of your strength, you need to master tension.

TENSION TECHNIQUES

Once you get used to the idea that your fingers are connected to your toes and that connection is important, you start to pay attention. A strong lower body - all people have a lower body that is stronger than their upper - can only be useful if you master tension. Not only can you transfer energy more effectively, through tension you can create a sense of strength that you never have had.

The structure of the human body is well-supported by the bones, except in the midsection. From the hips to the ribs we have nothing but a stick of little discs. By creating a high level of pressure with the muscles of the diaphragm and the air held in the lungs, we can keep these discs safe, and transfer power well from the legs to the arms.

Although we have known about tension in one form or another for years, from bracing in a heavy lift or holding breath during exertion, we didn't really have a grasp on it until we began learning kettlebell training with the organization Strong First. At the Strong

First seminars, the participants are asked to complete very difficult tasks with kettlebells, and through mastering tension, many of them set personal-best records at the event.

The tension techniques are described below. Although each one of these is effective in its own right, the combination of several (or all) of them is when you'll really see big results. Some of these can be hard to master - be patient, practice, and keep working on it, and you'll see yourself get stronger long after the muscles are maxed out.

THE BREATHING MATCH

The biomechanical breathing match is all about harnessing the power of your breath - via creating tension in the diaphragm. By increasing intra-abdominal pressure, we not only can integrate the power of our full body, but we also reduce the risk of injury. With this technique the exerciser breathes in with flexion and exhales powerfully with extension. For example, when pressing a weight overhead from shoulder height, you would exhale sharply as the weight passes the height of the ear, and then inhale as the weight is lowered or with the weight held in the bottom position.

Similarly, one would breathe deeply before descending into a squat, bracing the core tightly at the bottom of the movement, and then exhale sharply to begin the ascent. These are partial breaths, not full belly exhalations.

This technique is borrowed from martial arts; imagine how a fighter must hold his core tight while fighting close, knowing that a punch to a soft core could mean a knockdown...or worse.

To practice this technique, assume a position sitting upright on the floor or in a chair. Sitting as tall as possible, draw in a full breath through the nose, then make some short quick exhales through the mouth, making a "tsss" sound. Match each exhale with a short inhale back through the nose. So, it goes, "tsss", snort in some air, "tsss", snort, etc. You should be exhaling forcefully enough with each exhale that you can feel the abs contract when pressing your fingertips into your belly. Climbers tend to laugh at the forced breathing and yelling made by top-level climbers, but these behaviors are fundamental to high force generation.

By avoiding a full exhalation we never let the core go soft and can sustain very high loads an well as exploit the full potential of our total body strength.

IRRADIATION

Irradiation is the activation of additional muscles around the working muscle that "augments postural stability and enables the transfer of power across joints by two-joint muscles," according to Dr. Roger Inoka. You can experience this by simply trying to make a fist as tight as you can. If you really try to make it tight, you'll use not only the flexors of the forearm, but will feel yourself flex the extensors, the biceps, and probably your abs.

Not only does this help stabilize the working joints, it also increases nerve impulses to the working muscle, effectively making it stronger. We use this technique frequently when doing single-arm work. To test it, pick a dumbbell or kettlebell up and bring it to the shoulder, ready to press it overhead. As you get ready to press, though, concentrate on squeezing the non-working hand into a tight fist while pressing the weight overhead with the other arm. Due to irradiation of motor overflow, crushing with the hand increases one's strength in most strength efforts.

This is a natural part of climbing (we are almost always irradiating between the hands and feet while we grip the wall), and so, too, should be part of your supplemental training.

CRACK THE NUT

The glutes are the strongest and largest muscles in your body. They are a primary mover in most total-body exercises, from deadlifts to pull-ups, and they are somewhat neglected by this generation of athletes. We are not advocating going on a butt-focused training plan, but rather learning to use this already-strong group of muscles to increase your strength. If you can envision your glutes as the foundation of your core, you'll get a lot more out of every core exercise.

When performing difficult upper body exercises, notably overhead presses or pulling motions, maintaining tight glutes will help you harness the strength of your lower body and will prevent "energy leaks" such as swaying hips or and over-arched low back. To get a feel for this, stand tall with your feet squarely placed under the shoulders. With an upright posture, squeeze the glutes together; early on we jokingly encouraged our students to imagine cracking a walnut between their glutes...and the image stuck. Whether you like this image or not, focus on a tight abdominal wall, standing tall and squeezing the glutes together.

FOOT DRIVE

Foot drive, consciously pushing the feet into the floor when lifting weights overhead, has long been a helpful cue for generating more force when training. In climbing, actively pushing your feet down onto the holds creates more power from the legs, and reduces load on the arms.

Many of us tend to try to climb straight-armed in an effort to conserve energy in the arms. This works very well in long-endurance efforts, but the relaxation of the arms can also tend to encourage sagging at the hips. To help climbers understand the necessity of core tension, we do a simple demo. Take a bathroom scale and place it on the floor below your hangboard. It should be about 12-16" behind the plane of the board to better simulate overhanging terrain.

Next, hang from the board with straight arms, and place both feet on the scale, but think of staying relaxed and just hanging

your torso from the board with loose hips. Note the weight shown on the scale - for most of us, it will be around 30-50 pounds (14-22kg). Now tighten the hips and try to drive the feet onto the scale. At this point the weight shown on the scale will more than double, and since there is no change in the load, we can safely assume that this increase in weight on the feet is a decrease in the arms.

By practicing continued dedication to foot drive, we can increase endurance, but we can also increase total body power. By creating a strong pillar from the toes to the tips of the fingers, we learn to use the force of our whole body rather than just that of the arms when the going gets tough. The body has almost an infinite capacity for force production in a climbing-like situation, and the arms have very little on their own.

BRACING

For several years, starting in maybe the late 1980s, there was a tendency among trainers and coaches to cue "drawing in" the navel when lifting heavy. The idea was that the athlete would then be recruiting the transversus abdominis muscles and would thus be more stable in the core. The truth is that although this worked to some degree, the bracing of the core can be a far more natural - and effective - action.

Get ready to be punched in the stomach. This simple cue gets almost every athlete into the proper braced mode, and avoids unnatural spinal alignment, over-contraction, and confusion. A great way to get a feel for the bracing is to do a pull-up series. On the first pull-up, try to keep your hips loose and legs relaxed. This will probably feel really strange and unnatural. If so, you're probably already bracing to some degree.

Next, we'll over-emphasize the abs by holding an "L" position in the pull-up. This over-contraction will highlight that too much abdominal contraction can be counter-productive. Trying to do even half as many pull-ups as we normally can do while in the L is very difficult. Finally, set-up for the pull, hold the glutes tight (see Crack the Nut, above) and brace the abs as if you're about to be punched. This is the optimum situation for maximizing your pulls.

POSTURE

To generate the greatest force with the lowest risk of injury, you want to make sure you are structurally aligned. A simple cue for this comes from physical therapist Gray Cook: Holding correct body position in climbing is key, but trying to tell someone how to do it is terribly difficult. Short of coaching it move for move, and thus giving the climber way too many movement schemas, we've found that reminding our climbers to be "tall and skinny" usually cleans up most movement errors.

Tall and skinny forces you to hold a tight core, keep good posture in your back, and use your legs. The best way to practice this is in the warm-ups. Set a timer to chime every minute. During your warm-up climbing (say 10-15 minutes) you'll go tall and skinny each time you hear the timer chime. Over time, you'll see that you don't have to correct as often, and eventually, won't have to correct ever.

An additional postural cue has to do with neck alignment. Many young athletes are cued to look up at the ceiling during deadlifts or squats. This large-group cue comes from the coaches' desire to keep the team from rounding forward into lumbar extension and risking back injuries. Although a hyperextended neck might help with the low back issue, it is far from ideal. Research (and practical application) shows that simply keeping the neck aligned with the rest of the spine is the safest position, and allows for the greatest force production.

TIMING

Getting your muscles tight at the right time is also a key. To some degree, activation is intuitive. However, many novice athletes tend to initiate movement from the "outside in" rather than starting from the core. When setting up for a hard move or a difficult lift, think of starting with your abdominals braced first, then priming the main muscles for the movement and finally the grip or foot placement. In time, these won't be separated parts of movement, but will flow together in a matter of milliseconds.

This is an important building block to setting up for hard moves, but is also key in "starting strength" - going from unloaded to fully engaged under high force.

"WATER TO STATUE"

Martial arts great Bruce Lee talked about flowing from a liquid state to a solid, like "water to statue." Although a martial arts technique, the idea in climbing is the same. We go from being very relaxed and loose (and capable of generating lots of speed) to being completely rigid and holding a maximal isometric position instantly.

Many climbers are too tight in the flow of movement and too loose when they engage at the end of a move. When it comes time to pull hard on small holds or move heavy weight quickly, we need to be able to work to both extremes. By mastering relaxation moments at a time - as we do between moves - we can enhance not only our ability to exert power, but our ability to endure several hard moves in a row.

STRENGTH EXERCISES

The strength exercises in this book are selected based on their usefulness for climbing, their ease of implementation in a variety of facilities, and on their simplicity to learn. These exercises are not a replacement for specific exercises used for climbing, but are, as we stated on the cover of this book, a foundation for better implementation of skill training. There are many exercises not included here, and many of those can be excellent choices in your training. Understanding where your exercises will fit into our programs is very simple, as all of the exercises you could possibly do can be categorized by *movement pattern*. Once you know which movement pattern an exercise fits in, it is simple enough to plug it in to any training plan.

MOVEMENT PATTERNS, NOT MUSCLE GROUPS

Our general strength exercises are used to increase overall strength and are not necessarily specific to climbing. These are familiar exercises and all of them are done either with bodyweight or with weight training equipment. We have categorized these exercises by movement pattern rather than by "muscle group", as isolating a movement to a particular group can be difficult, and is somewhat useless for an athlete. The exercises we recommend are almost all multi-joint exercises that require many muscles working together to produce force. This stands in sharp contrast to the bodybuilding style of weight training where one performs isolative exercises on individual muscle groups.

The goal of our training sessions is to increase strength, optimally doing so without adding additional muscle mass. Our exercises are selected with this in mind. In the following pages, we'll detail exercises from 5 major movement patterns: Upper Body Press, Upper Body Pull, Lower Body Hip Hinge, Lower Body Squat, and Core.

This list is by no means exhaustive. We eliminated a lot of great exercises from our programs over the years. Our whole goal is to build strength in climbers, but not the wrong kind. It doesn't matter at all what a climber can do in a given exercise if it doesn't make him better on the rock. We picked our exercises based on safety and ease of learning. In the following pages, we provide basic descriptions and photos of the exercises. We will also discuss how to best make exercises easier or more difficult to better suit your training - progression is not limited to simply adding more weight!

PROGRESSING AND REGRESSING EXERCISES

Every movement pattern we use in resistance training can be regressed or progressed to best suit the athlete. Early on, an athlete might lack the strength or skill to do the prescribed movement or exercise. Instead of simply using less weight or a shorter range of motion, the athlete can regress the movement to a simpler version. These simpler versions are designed to enhance skills and strength so that the climber can eventually progress to the harder versions of the moves.

Most of our programming in this book will suggest an anchor exercise for the movement. If you don't know how to do this movement, you simply need to regress it to a simpler version that you know, then work back toward doing the anchor exercise. Likewise, if you are an advanced trainee, you might want to progress an exercise so that it remains challenging for you where the anchor exercise might not.

Example progression and regression in the upper body pull:

2ND REGRESSION	1ST REGRESSION	ANCHOR EXERCISE	1ST PROGRESSION	2ND PROGRESSION
Pull Down	1/2 Chin	Pull-Up	L-Pull-up	Weighted Pull-Up

There are a number of ways to progress and regress movements, some better than others. In general, we want to keep the movement as similar to the anchor movement as possible. For example, many people that cannot do a regular push-up will try to make the movement easier by either doing the exercise with the knees on the ground or by doing a partial range-of-motion. Don't underestimate the value of the regressions. These are not a commentary on your ability, they are building blocks to successful progression to the more complex versions of the exercises.

Knee Push-Up / Partial Push-Up
Start

Knee Push-Up / Partial Push-Up
Bottom

Neither of these is ideal. The knee push-up diminishes the core tension component of the movement, while the partial range push-up eliminates sections of the exercise where the athlete most needs to develop strength. Instead, the regression should be a push-up in an inclined position, with the hands placed on a bench, chair, or even countertop - raising the upper body high enough that the full range can be performed with no errors in movement.

Incline Push-Up
Start

Incline Push-Up
Bottom

These progressions and regressions are listed on the next page and will be detailed in the exercise descriptions that follow.

EXERCISES BY MOVEMENT PATTERN

We have categorized the strength movements in this section into five patterns, as discussed earlier: Hip Hinge, Squat, Upper Body Press, Upper Body Pull, and Core. There are hundreds of good exercises that fit these categories, yet we will detail only a few - the ones we find most applicable to climbing and simple to perform with commonly available equipment. Naturally, experienced athletes may have other exercises they prefer. We urge you, however, to stick with the patterns, loading recommendations, and volume of training we suggest in order to get the most out of these sessions.

		<	REGRESSION	MOVEMENT PATTERN	PROGRESSION	>	
	Glute Bridge	Kettlebell Deadlift	Kettlebell Swing	**HIP HINGE**	Trap Bar Deadlift	Barbell RDL	Barbell Deadlift
Assisted Split Squat	Split Squat	Goblet Squat	Air Squat	**SQUAT**	Weighted Lunge	Two KB Rack Squat	Barbell Front Squat
	One-Arm Half Kneeling Landmine Press	One-Arm Standing Landmine Press	One-Arm Military Press	**VERTICAL PRESS**	Two-Arm Military Press	One-Arm Push Press	Two-Arm Push Press
Incline Push-Up	Push-Up	One-Arm Dumbbell Bench or Floor Press	Two-Arm Floor Press	**HORIZONTAL PRESS**	Bench Press	One-Arm Push-Up	One-Arm One-Leg Push-Up
Lat Pull-Down	Pull-Up Regressions (p. 184-185)	Pull-Up	Tactical Pull-Up	**VERTICAL PULL**	L-Sit Pull-Up	Weighted Pull-Up	Towel Pull-Up
		Inverted Row	One-Arm Inverted Row	**HORIZONTAL PULL**	One-Arm Dumbbell Row	Standing Two-Arm Dumbbell or Barbell Row	

		<	REGRESSION	CORE EXERCISE	PROGRESSION	>
Hanging Knee Raise	Hanging Straight Leg Raise		Seated Straight Leg Raise	**STRAIGHT LEG RAISE**	Ankles to Bar	Hanging Straight Leg Raise (Start with Hips at 90°)
		Physioball Roll-Out On Knees	Physioball Roll-Out On Feet	**ROLL-OUT**	Ab Wheel Roll-Out On Knees	Ab Wheel Roll-Out On Feet
		Assisted Front Lever (Feet in Resistance Band)	One-Leg Tucked Front Lever	**FRONT LEVER**	Front Lever	Front Lever (Slower Reps or with Isometric Hold at Top)

Please note, this is not a comprehensive list of all the lifts for each movement pattern, but a tool for progressing your lifts to harder and harder versions. This is also not a list of which exercise is better. These exercises are for athletes depending on ability and the goal of the training session. You also might notice, some of these lifts are not explained in the book.

THE HIP HINGE

The hip hinge is the most underutilized major movement pattern in the gym. This isn't a knock to general gym goers, it's just goes to show how hard this movement is to learn and how unnatural it feels when first performed. Most climbers have squatted some weight or even gone to the bathroom in the woods, pressed some weight up overhead that one time they put a mattress on their vehicle, and rattled off a few pull-ups on a buddy's pull-up bar. It's rare to find an athlete getting into training for the first time who has performed a correct hip hinge or even know what one looks like. The hip hinge is the way we should pick things up off the floor, but most of us just fold forward or squat.

The hip hinge targets a very important area of the body, the lower back, the glutes, and the hamstrings. Together these are known as the posterior chain or the "back abs." Working the hip hinge is very subtle and can sometimes looks like a squat, but is defined as having the hips above the knees, the shoulders above the hips, and the shins near vertical.

While keeping your neck and spine neutral, you want to pretend like your hips are on a fixed track and all they do is move back and forth horizontally...not up and down. Of course there may be some degree of up and down (depending on how you're built or what variation of the hinge you'll be doing), but the first cue is hips back and then you can adjust from there. Compared to a squat, your hips will hardly lose any elevation in the hip hinge.

For example, the deadlift start position can look different depending on how you're built. The angle of hips, knees, and arms can be totally different from person to person based on femur, torso, and arm length. Some deadlift positions look a bit more like a squat (hips low) while others look more like a romanian deadlift (hips high). It just depends on how you fit into the start position.

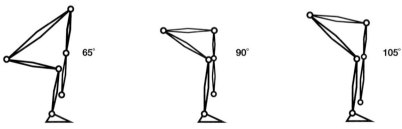

Adapted from a Mark Rippetoe illustration.

Regardless of your start position there are a few things that remain true:

- Shins are near vertical or vertical
- Hips are above the knees
- Shoulder are above the hips
- Spine and neck are neutral

DEADLIFT

BARBELL DEADLIFT

The deadlift is pure strength. There is no cheating the range of motion - you pull from the ground and you don't dare stop until you are standing. Although it works the legs, it is primarily a "posterior chain" exercise, taxing the hamstrings, glutes, and muscles of the low back. For building pure total body strength, no exercise comes close.

The stance should be shoulder width apart or slightly narrower with your toes slightly kicked outward or neutral. The hips should be above your knees and your shoulders above your hips. The shins should be near vertical and the barbell should be touching your shins. The grip is outside your stance, somewhere around shoulder width apart. The head, neck, and spine are neutral. Before you lift, take the "slack" out of the bar. This means tense your whole body like you're going to lift the bar, but don't. Have a proud chest, squeeze the barbell, flex your lats, and fire your glutes. As you pull the barbell up your shins, the hips and shoulders rise simultaneously while keeping a neutral spine. At the top, completely lock out the deadlift by squeezing your glutes, your quads and holding your core rigid. Reverse the movement and once the barbell gets past your knees you can drop it to the floor.

BARBELL DROP

This is where we see the majority of deadlifting injuries, the last 10 percent of the lift. As the lifter brings the weight back down, their back is in its most vulnerable position between the knees and the floor, especially as a lifter fatigues. If lifting correctly, an athlete can certainly keep the barbell in their hands and rattle off more reps, but once the load gets heavy or you're going for a 1 rep max, the risk to reward benefit is marginal, at best. Additionally, climbers are not concerned with the eccentric movement of the deadlift (Bringing the barbell back down to the floor).

We are using this lift for the benefits of the concentric movement (Bringing the barbell from the floor to the top position). When lifting at maximal loads it's common practice to drop the barbell once you clear the knees. Please make sure you are dropping weights that were meant to be dropped (i.e. bumper plates - as soon in photos). Most gyms have bumper plates and rubber floors for this exact reason. If you belong to a gym that doesn't allow you to drop weights, find another gym. OK, that may not be realistic, but consider finding another gym that allows you to do this. There really are gyms out there that don't allow you to drop weights. I know the steam room, hot tub, and spa are awesome perks of said gym, but are they making you stronger? Think about it.

GRIP

Both palms facing you is the most common grip and the one that should be used most of the time when deadlifting.

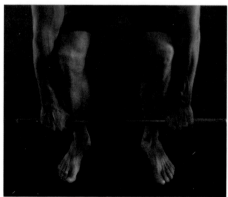

BB Deadlift
Close-Up Hand Position

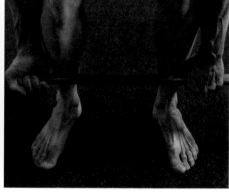

BB Deadlift
Close-Up Mixed Grip

You also might try the mixed grip. This grip is primarily used when trying maximal loads. It feels a bit awkward at first, but it's a strong grip. If you are going for a big lift, your dominant hand should be palm back and the other hand will be palm forward. You can train heavy loads with this grip, but make sure you switch the grip between sets. (i.e. Set 1 - left palm facing forward and Set 2 - left palm facing back)

BB Deadlift Start

BB Deadlift Halfway

BB Deadlift Finish

BB Finish (Side)

GO SETS VERSUS STOP SETS

The deadlift can be an exceedingly taxing exercise and can be dangerous if your form comes apart. People will claim they injured themselves deadlifting, when the reality is that they injured themselves by deadlifting poorly. With this in mind, we often prescribe Stop Sets in the deadlift, where the athlete pulls the weight from the ground under strict control and with perfect form, then returns it to the ground and stands up without the bar for a moment before doing a second pull. In effect this looks like several sets of single reps with a short, 5-10 second rest between. Each Stop Set forces you to work that difficult starting strength every single rep, and can be a useful and safer variation to the lift.

Go Sets are normal sets of reps, where the weight is lifted and lowered in a normal fashion at a fixed tempo. In Go Sets, the posterior chain is not completely unloaded, and thus retains some elastic energy to help with subsequent reps.

KB DEADLIFT

The Kettlebell Deadlift is performed with either one or two kettlebells placed between the feet. The movement is a "sumo" style pull, but is slightly different than the Sumo Deadlift done with a barbell. The set-up for the kettlebell deadlift is similar to the normal start, except your feet are just slightly wider than shoulder width apart, and the kettlebell(s) is placed between the balls of the feet. Look forward (not down...the kettlebell will not have moved) and reach down for the bell with arms locked straight - almost as if you were trying to cramp the triceps. Don't squat down, but rather push the hips back, forcing your hamstrings to tighten up. Once your hands are on the bell, tighten up the system - feet "grab" the floor, glutes flex, abs braced for a punch, hands crushing the bell handle, and...

Pull the bell off the floor by pushing your hips forward. Your arms will slide up the inside of your thighs, and as you straighten up you'll exhale a little air. It's important to "hiss" the air out. Too much exhalation will let you lose some core tension. Stand up tall at the top. You should look like you're having your height measured, not like you're leading into a back bend.

KB Deadlift Start   KB Deadlift Start

KB Deadlift Halfway   KB Finish

TRAP BAR DEADLIFT

The Trap Bar is a barbell with a diamond or hexagonal space in the middle, in which the lifter will stand. It allows the deadlift to be performed with less forward lean, and is frequently used as an instructional tool for new lifters. We also like trap bar deadlifting as a variation to the hard pulling of the traditional deadlift.

To start, step inside the trap bar. With feet slightly narrower than shoulder width apart, hinge at the hips until you can reach the handles. The arm position on the trap bar is wide, so many athletes will need to drop the body lower than in a normal deadlift. Drive the hips back and try to maintain as vertical a shin as possible. Keep the neck neutral and eyes on the floor in front of you.

Tighten the glutes, and with a "proud" chest pull the bar off the floor slowly. Jerking the bar tends to cause your back to lose stiffness. Although you'll be able to "squat" more in this variation, keep in mind that the end goal is to deadlift more effectively, so keep focusing on the hinge. Continue the pull until you are upright and the knees are locked straight. To reverse the move, inhale, set the abs, and drive it carefully back to the ground.

Trap Bar DL	Trap Bar DL	Trap Bar DL
Start	Halfway	Finish

SUMO DEADLIFT

The Sumo Deadlift is a barbell deadlift done with the same basic body position as the kettlebell deadlift explained earlier. Again, the main difference between this and the traditional deadlift is the outward knee position and the tracking of the arms inside the knees. The Sumo Deadlift allows for a more upright position, and is easier for some body types. Because this variant uses more leg strength and less low back strength, it is not the preferred variation for our purposes - we look to the deadlift as a core tension exercise more than a leg strengthener.

Place the feet with heels at least shoulder-width apart. Roll the bar back until it touches the inside of the shins. Squat down to the bar, the grab hold with the arms parallel and the elbows (obviously) between the knees. Lock the bar into place by trying to "point the elbows backward." Make sure the spine is tight and the neck is held in a neutral alignment.

Tighten the glutes, and with a "proud" chest pull the bar off the floor slowly. Jerking the bar tends to cause your back to lose stiffness. Continue the pull until you are upright and the knees are locked straight. To reverse the move, inhale, set the abs, and drive it carefully back to the ground.

Sumo DL
Start

Sumo DL
Halfway

Sumo DL
Finish

ROMANIAN DEADLIFT

The Romanian Deadlift, also known as the stiff legged deadlift, is one where we are using the hamstrings as the primary mover. The quads are taken out of the equation by only allowing a slight knee bend or none at all, thus you'll use less weight than a traditional deadlift. Shoot your hips back, as you do in any hip hinge movement, but this time keep your legs straight as possible or have a slight knee bend. Concentrate on hinging from the hips as much as you can until you reach down to the bar. However, your back must remain neutral, no rounded backs here.

The back should be parallel to the ground. If you can reach the bar with straight legs and a neutral back, great. If not, your hamstring mobility is the limiting factor and you should not pull from the ground because you'll have no choice but to pull with a compromised spine. What you'll do instead, is pull a normal deadlift off the ground to the top position. When you go down for the next rep you'll assume the stiff legged position. Only go down as far as you can without rounding your back. As soon as you reach that point, mostly likely above the floor and just below your knees, you'll come back up. In trying to hold the knees straight, make sure the knees don't drift back past the plane of the heels. Don't sacrifice your spine just to touch the floor. You can elevate the bar on blocks if you want a target to hit for each rep.

You'll want to revert back to a traditional deadlift so pay attention. It's understandable because the traditional deadlift feels strong and more natural, but fight the urge. This lift really focuses on the hamstrings and it will feel awkward at first. The most important part is shooting your butt back as far as you can at the bottom while keeping a neutral spine and straight legs. As you pull keep the barbell over your feet and pull your hips back to center. At the top of the lift make sure you complete the rep by locking your whole body out at the top.

| Romanian Deadlift Start | Romanian Deadlift Halfway | Romanian Deadlift Finish |

SWING

TWO-ARM SWING

We use kettlebell swings with almost all of our athletes, almost all the time. The kettlebell swing is a great exercise for lower body power development and integration of movement. Start with the kettlebell on the ground a foot or more in front of you, then reach down and "hike" the bell back to start the reps. Think "thumbs to bum" as the KB passes through the legs rather than swinging it low between the knees. When swinging, only squat enough to get the bell between the legs (handle passing above the knees) and snap the hips forward to raise the kettlebell to the height of the sternum. The bell should not be lifted by the arms, but rather shot forward by the hips. Picture the arms as ropes or chains rather than levers.

Swinging higher in the so-called "American swing" actually diminishes the power component of the exercise, making it an easy knee-dominant movement instead of a hip dominant move. Many coaches caution against swinging overhead due to the dynamic lumbar flexion that most athletes exhibit at the top of the move.

A great cue for knowing when to hinge is to imagine you're in waist deep water. As you begin your swing the hips should be in full extension before the bells comes out of the water (Look at photo). Then, after the float at the top position, let the bell fall and hinge when the bell hits that water. This does two things. For one it gives you a good solid powerful swing and it also helps prevent you from experiencing lower back pain if you're hinging too early. You want to feel like you're playing chicken with the kettlebell. Be patient.

| KB Swing Hike | KB Swing Between Legs | KB Swing Halfway | KB Swing Finish |

ONE-ARM SWING

This single arm kettlebell swing is a good hip-hinge drill, but really is more effective as a core anti-rotation exercise. This movement requires additional recruitment of muscles compared to the standard swing. The set-up and movement should exactly mimic the two-hand swing, but you will only hold the bell in one hand. It is especially key to focus on holding the shoulders packed and squared up with the hips, even as the momentum of the bell tries to force you to rotate "open."

When hiking the bell from the ground, grab the handle of the bell loosely, with the hand in the very middle of the handle. Take the slack out of the system, tighten your grip, and start your hike pass. Hold the shoulders square as the bell passes behind the legs, and maintain that tension as you stand up into the top position.

| 11Arm KB Swing Hike | 1-Arm KB Swing Hike | 1-Arm KB Swing Between Legs | 1-Arm KB Swing Finish |

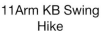

WHAT TO DO WITH YOUR NONWORKING ARM

Let's take a moment and talk about what to do with your non-working arm. There are two types of kettlebell lifts - ballistics and grinds. Ballistics are explosive, like swings and cleans. Grinds are slow, like presses. Each require different techniques to give your other arm something to do. This isn't just busy work either. Employing the right techniques will actually make you stronger and more efficient, even though that arm isn't doing all the heavy lifting.

We'll start with ballistics. Let's take the one arm swing for example. You should always start a one arm swing with both hands on the kettlebell. Why? This will square your shoulders and you won't start off in bad form before you even start. Right before you hike the kettlebell between your legs, you'll let your non-working arm drift off to the side. Make a fist and clench. Think of your arm being inline with your torso. As you swing, think of the non-working arm mirroring the working arm. It goes up, it goes down. All in one fluid motion. It's just like a shadow or that annoying brother who keeps following you around.

By mirroring the other arm you'll keep your shoulders square throughout the arc of the swing. By keeping your shoulders square, you'll avoid rotation of your neck, back, and spine. You don't have to be a rocket scientist to understand that rotating your torso with a heavy load, moving at high speeds, in varying planes, may be bit of a problem. Don't be a wet noodle.

At the top of the swing there are two types of finishes. The first way is to have your non-working arm finish the same way your working arm does at the top of the swing. Both arms out in front. Think vertical palm plank. The other way, is to finish your non-working arm in the "fighter" pose. As your non-working arm comes up past your hips, instead of letting it float out in front of you, you'll tuck your arm in close to your chest and make a fist. Think of how a boxer looks in the ring.

Now for the kettlebell press (p.181), or a what we would call a grind.

Instead of letting your hand do whatever it feels like, you should close the 'strength loop' by making a fist and send more strength to the loaded arm. This is called muscle irradiation. If you create more tension in other muscle groups that energy will spill over and make you stronger and more stable.

In short, there are a few key muscle groups that you want to fire when pressing weight overhead or for any big lifts (squats, deadlift, turkish get-up, etc). The forearms, abs, glutes, and quads. By tensing all these muscle groups, it makes the Central Nervous System (CNS) feel safe and you'll generate more power (p.134).

CLEAN (ONE AND TWO-ARM)

The kettlebell clean is the easiest and safest way to bring kettlebells from the floor to rack position at the shoulder. It is a precursor to the squat, press and other exercises where the bells start at the shoulder. This can be done with either one or two kettlebells, and the technique is the same.

Start as you would for a kettlebell swing, in the standard "hike" position. Swing the bell/bells back, but as the kettlebells swing forward, be sure to pin the elbows to the side of the ribs and shorten the arc. As the kettlebells pass the hip, snap them into rack position in the crook of your arms. To return the bells to the ground, simply reverse the movement.

1-Arm KB Clean
Hike

1-Arm KB Clean
Hike

1-Arm KB Clean
Between Legs

1-Arm KB Clean
Halfway

1-Arm KB Clean
Finish

1-Arm KB Clean
Finish

This can be a bit uncomfortable at first, but with practice becomes smooth and simple. If your arms are bruised or your forearms are hurting after training this movement, you are doing it wrong and should seek out qualified coaching.

LEVER

Front Lever
Finish

Front Lever
Finish

Although the lever is frequently regarded as a core or abdominal exercise, it is in fact a quasi-isometric hip hinge exercise. There is no arguing the abs are used in the movement, but the glutes, lats, and spinal erectors bear the majority of the load. This is an excellent exercise for all levels of climbers, and can be progressed or regressed very well. The simplest regression involves the use of an elastic band assist, the hardest, simply bodyweight.

BAND-ASSISTED LEVER

Although there are several regressions taught for the lever, the one we see the most success with is the band-assisted lever. In this variation, you'll girth-hitch a elastic training band (usually a 36-40 inch rubber band .75" to 2" in thickness) to a pull-up bar. If your gym doesn't have these, you can either find a new gym or buy them yourself. Both Rogue Fitness (www.roguefitness.com) and Perform Better (www.performbetter.com) sell very good ones.

While holding onto the bar or an upright for balance, place BOTH FEET in the bottom of the band loop. Hold onto the bar with one hand on each side of the band, then try to *press the bar down* while lifting your rigid lower body to a horizontal position. It is critical not to try to raise the feet as you would in a straight leg raise, but rather to lift the hips.

Move slowly and in full control to the top position and then reverse slowly to the start. Once you can complete 5 full slow reps with a given band, reduce the band width by ¼" and try again. Once you are working with a ½" band, it's time to move up to a Single-Leg Tuck Lever.

Band-Assisted Lever Start   Band-Assisted Lever Halfway   Band-Assisted Lever Finish

SINGLE-LEG TUCK LEVER

The first bodyweight progression of the lever is really the two-leg tuck lever, better known as knees-to-elbows. You should be able to complete five good, clean reps of this exercise before moving on to the single-leg tuck. To do the single-leg tuck, assume the starting position on the pull-up bar, then tuck one leg up as close to the chest as possible, while at the same time locking the lats in to drive the hips up. Lever up to a top position where the body and extended leg are completely horizontal. Watch for sagging hips here - this error must be corrected immediately or you should regress to an easier version for a few weeks to build up the strength.

Return slowly to the bottom position, being careful to try and keep the pace as slow as the ascent phase was.

Single Leg Tuck Lever
Start

Single Leg Tuck Lever
Finish

STRAIGHT LEVER

The straight lever is the ultimate bodyweight hip-hinge exercise. Place the hands slightly wider than shoulder-width apart on a pull-up bar. Hold onto the bar with an exaggerated crushing grip, then try to press the bar down while lifting your rigid lower body to a horizontal position. It is critical not to try to raise the feet as you would in a straight leg raise, but rather to lift the hips.

Move slowly and in full control to the top position and then reverse slowly to the start. Once you can complete 5 full slow reps, you are not only a badass, but you should advance into doing even slower reps.

Front Lever
Start

Front Lever
Halfway

Front Lever
Finish

Front Lever
Finish

THE SQUAT

Goblet Squat
Bottom

Most people have done some sort of squat in their lives. When we were babies, our squat was amazing. Our hips were nice and flexible, we had a good strength to weight ratio, and the deep squat was how we would pick things up off the ground or even play with toys. This is a skill that is lost as we age, and is difficult to recoup. Squatting is the major movement pattern responsible for strengthening the quadriceps and is a *knee dominant* exercise. The biggest limiter for most athletes is tight hip flexors and a weak core. These weaknesses are illuminated when asked to do a squat at bodyweight. If you simply can't get your thighs parallel to the floor without picking your heels off the ground or folding forward at the waist, you have some work to do.

The squat is defined as keeping tall spine throughout the entire lift. As you descend, keep a tight midsection as you pull yourself down into position until the hips are just past the knees, keep tight and come up out of the hole all the way to the top. Finish the squat with flexed quads, glutes and core. Described below are several variations on this theme. Split position squats will be easier for less-mobile athletes, and are a good place to start.

LUNGE

The lunge pattern is a split-position squat where one foot is placed slightly in front of the hips and the other 16-20" behind. From this pattern, we can do a split-squat (leaving the feet in place and moving up and down), a lunge (moving dynamically through the range), or even a walking lunge.

Bodyweight Lunge
Bottom

SPLIT SQUAT

Most adults don't have the mobility to squat correctly without some amount of training. In order to train strength effectively until that mobility comes, we often put our athletes in a split-stance position. From split squats, to lunges, to step-ups, training one leg at a time is both effective in building strength and very specific to sports movement.

Assuming a split position, simply descend straight down to a position where the back knee hovers approximately 1-2 inches from the floor. Pressing equally with both legs, return to the top position.

Assisted Split-Squat
Start

Assisted Split-Squat
Bottom

Bodyweight Split Squat
Start

Bodyweight Split Squat
Bottom

LUNGE / BACK LUNGE / WALKING LUNGE

Keeping an upright spine, step forward into a full lunge, with the trailing knee held 1 to 2 inches from the floor. When doing lunges in place, you'll lunge back to the start position. The back lunge differs in that you'll keep the front foot planted, and lunge backward into the bottom position with the other leg. This variant is a bit more stable, and is somewhat more sport-specific than the traditional lunge. When doing a walking lunge, step forward out of the lunge directly into a lunge with the other leg. Add resistance by holding dumbbells or kettlebells in the hands. A more intense variation is to hold the kettlebells in rack position during the course of the exercise.

| Weighted Lunge Start | Weighted Lunge Step | Weighted Lunge Halfway | Weighted Lunge Bottom |

| Weighted Back Lunge Start | Weighted Back Lunge Halfway | Weighted Back Lunge Bottom |

| Weighted Walking Lunge Start | Weighted Walking Lunge Step | Weighted Walking Lunge Halfway | Weighted Walking Lunge Bottom |

SINGLE LEG SQUAT

The single-leg squat is the top of the food chain in leg training for climbers. It requires high levels of strength, but also a tremendous amount of balance and mobility. It is a motorically difficult movement, and is often enough of a challenge at first to discourage athletes from continuing to practice. Over time, this should become a staple in your training.

Start by standing on a box or bench at least 16" high. Turn so that one leg is held in the air to the side of the box, and the inside of the planted foot is right at the edge of the box. Although this exercise can be done at bodyweight, it is actually easier to start with a little weight in the hands to help with balance at the bottom of the movement. A pair of 5# weights is probably about right for most athletes to start with.

Sit back, and as your hips drop, raise the weights up to shoulder-height out in front of you. Squat down until your calf touches your glute - much lower than you would take a normal 2-leg squat. Concentrate on keeping the heel planted and drive the movement from there.

Progress this exercise by adding a little weight to the dumbbells. Once your bells are over about 15 pounds, this becomes problematic. If you get this strong, the exercise should be progressed to a pistol squat or you should add weight with a vest.

ASSISTED SINGLE LEG SQUAT

For athletes who can't quite get the single-leg squat at bodyweight, an excellent regression is to have them assist the movement with the arms. There are two primary ways we address this: either using a TRX / set of rings, or by holding onto an upright, such as a squat rack in the gym. When using an arm assist, a very useful rule is to try and maintain the same position as you might in a bodyweight squat - upright position, proud chest, maximum forward position.

Holding onto the strap or upright, descend straight down, working on maximum flexion of the ankle, and upon reaching the bottom position (hamstring touching calf) try to release your grip a bit to test stability. If you fall back, it is probably an inflexible ankle or hip more than bad balance. Once you can do five reps with a given assist, go back to attempting the bodyweight or light-weight versions.

| Assisted Pistol Squat Start | Assisted Pistol Squat Halfway | Assisted Pistol Squat Bottom |

| Lightweight Pistol Squat Start | Lightweight Pistol Squat Halfway | Lightweight Pistol Squat Bottom |

Bodyweight
Pistol Squat
Start

Bodyweight
Pistol Squat
Halfway

Bodyweight
Pistol Squat
Bottom

Heavyweight
Pistol Squat
Start

Heavyweight
Pistol Squat
Bottom

GOBLET SQUAT

The goblet squat is a standard squat, yet performed with a dumbbell or kettlebell held in front of the chest. Hold the bell in front of the shoulders, either against the chest or a few inches away to help with balance. Maintain a full upright spine, and then squat down between the heels, keeping the chest proud until the elbows touch the inside of the knees. Once you hit the bottom position, drive back up to the top with no forward torso lean. Once the weight becomes difficult to manage, consider switching to a rack squat.

| Goblet Squat
Clean from Ground
Start | Goblet Squat
Clean from Ground
Halfway | Goblet Squat
Start |

| Goblet Squat
Start | Goblet Squat
Halfway | Goblet Squat
Bottom |

DOUBLE KETTLEBELL "RACK" SQUAT

The rack squat is a front squat done with kettlebells. As simple as this variation may seem, changing to kettlebells represents a substantial improvement in the movement for most athletes. Positioning the kettlebells in "the rack" forces a solid core and allows you to move quickly between exercises: cleaning the kettlebells and starting to squat is much faster and easier than setting up a squat bar.

Start with a pair of kettlebells placed side by side on the ground in front of you. Grab the handles and clean the bells to your shoulders (if you don't know the clean, now is the time to learn...see Kettlebell Clean p. 161). In rack, you should be standing tall, bells sitting in the crooks of your elbows, with the elbows held tight against the ribs. Forearms should be vertical, and wrists straight. Females might feel more comfortable with a wider elbow position and angled forearms to avoid having the kettlebells resting on the breasts.

The movement involves sitting "between the heels" and maintaining that good, upright position. This is an easier variant of the squat than most, and you should find full range of motion is easier than in the barbell variants. Look for a clean, smooth movement - if you have hitches in any part of the range of motion, back off a little on the weight. At the end of the set, reverse the clean (rather than dropping the bells in some weird side to side curl movement) and set the bells down.

| 2 KB Squat | 2 KB Squat | 2KB Squat |
| Start | Start | Bottom |

FRONT SQUAT

The front squat is a standard squat, yet performed with a barbell racked on the front of the shoulder rather than on the back. We prefer this variation to the back squat, both because it is easier to get away from the bar in a failed rep and because poor squat form makes the movement virtually impossible.

Front Squat Fail
Weight to Rack

Front Squat Fail
Weight to Floor

Hold the bar in front of the shoulders, letting it rest against the neck and sit on top of the deltoids. Maintain a full upright spine, and then squat down between the heels, keeping the chest proud and the elbows high in front of you. Once you hit the bottom position, drive back up to the top with no forward torso lean.

Occasionally, you will fail. This is why we love the front squat - if you fail at any point in the movement, it is easy to push the bar away and drop it on the floor. If you are lifting very heavy weight, consider squatting in a rack with spotting rails placed at appropriate height.

BB Front Squat
Start

BB Front Squat
Start

BB Front Squat
Halfway

BB Front Squat
Bottom

Some athletes experience discomfort in the wrists during this lift. If this is the case, try a looser grip on the bar, or consider the arms-crossed position. The latter compromises bar control, however, and should be used with caution.

BB Front Squat
Alternate Grip
Start

BB Front Squat
Alternate Grip
Bottom

THE PRESS

The upper body press is frequently overlooked by climbers, as it seems like it's not "sport specific." For years we programmed push-ups and overhead presses as injury-proofing antagonist movements, but as our involvement with competition climbers has advanced, we are seeing a greater and greater need for good total body strength to deal with the specific demands of that sport. There is simply much more pressing and counter-pressure movement in the sport than there was ten years ago.

The pressing exercises include all exercises that involve moving the body away from the implement (push-ups, dips) or moving the load away from the body (overhead press, bench press). Having a strong set of pressing muscles (primarily the deltoids and pectorals) will help prevent overuse injuries and can function to stabilize the joints of the shoulder and elbow.

PUSH-UP

The push-up is a well-known and widely practiced exercise that most of us have done hundreds of times. In our practice, we want to make the most of this simple exercise, so it might take a bit of relearning for some who have allowed compromised movement over the years.

Place the hands just slightly wider than shoulder width and hold the entire body tight - no sagging hips. The whole body must rise and fall at the same time. Lower the chest toward the floor, stopping with the chest about one inch from touching. Hold the neck in line with the back and look straight down or forward, not at the feet. Press back up to a straight-arm position at the top. No half push-ups. If you can't keep the lower half of your body connected to the upper half of your body you're not strong enough to be doing this exercise with the hands on the ground. If this is the case, regress to the incline push-up until you can keep a solid midsection. Same goes for flared elbows. If you can't do push-up with the elbows close to the body incline until you can. Elbow away from the body screams future shoulder injury.

| Bodyweight Push-Up | Bodyweight Push-Up | Bodyweight Push-Up |
| Start | Halfway | Bottom |

INCLINE PUSH-UP

The best regression for the standard push-up is the incline push-up. Instead of using the knees as the fulcrum as we see in the most popular regression, we suggest you put your hands on a box, bench, or countertop to decrease the load on the upper body. This is an excellent opportunity to practice the tight core and "pulling yourself down" into the bottom position. Once you can master 5-8 reps at a given incline, move down 4-6 inches and work at it again.

| Incline Push-Up | Incline Push-Up | Incline Push-Up |
| Start | Halfway | Bottom |

ONE-ARM PUSH-UP

People generally freak out when we tell them to do one-arm push-ups. This is a feat of great strength, and we all know it. There is a way to progress into the movement by inclining the upper body, and we've had great success in getting athletes to a full version on the ground with careful progression.

Start with your non-dominant hand on a countertop or box (In the gym, we like an Olympic bar placed in a rack at about waist height). Assume a solid foot stance, with feet slightly wider than shoulder width. Brace the abs actively as if readying for a punch in the stomach. Lower yourself into a full-range push-up, being sure to get the working hand within an inch or two of the chest. Press up under full control, then repeat the movement on the dominant side. As you master the prescribed reps (normally 3-5) at a given height, reduce the height of the implement by 2-3 inches, then work up to your max reps again.

Once you can do 5 solid reps on the ground, switch back to a slight incline and start working the 1-arm 1-leg push-up.

One-Arm
Incline Push-Up
Start

One-Arm
Incline Push-Up
Halfway

One-Arm
Incline Push-Up
Bottom

One-Arm Push-Up
Start

One-Arm Push-Up
Halfway

One-Arm Push-Up
Bottom

One-Arm, One-Leg
Incline Push-Up
Start

One-Arm, One-Leg
Incline Push-Up
Halfway

One-Arm, One-Leg
Incline Push-Up
Bottom

One-Arm, One-Leg
Push-Up
Start

One-Arm, One-Leg
Push-Up
Halfway

One-Arm, One-Leg
Push-Up
Bottom

OVERHEAD PRESS

The overhead press is a staple of upper body strength. Referred to as a "shoulder press" or as the "military press," this exercise is usually performed with a barbell or two handheld weights such as dumbbells or kettlebells. This is our favorite antagonist exercise for climbers as there is a big core stability component to the movement.

BARBELL PRESS

To begin the lift, safely bring the weight to shoulder height, either by picking it up from a rack or by cleaning the weight from the floor. With a tight core, tight glutes, and tight quads, take a short nasal inhalation, and then press the weight overhead with no hip displacement. Once the weight has cleared the level of the eyes/ears, let your breath out in a short hiss. Once the weight is locked overhead, return the weight to the starting position using the same control with which you pressed it.

BB Military Press
Start

BB Military Press
Halfway

BB Military Press
Finish

BB Military Press
Finish

KETTLEBELL SINGLE ARM AND 2-ARM PRESS

A more advanced movement, the kettlebell press involves significant core stability. We prefer the kettlebell for the overhead lift over dumbbells; the offset center of gravity helps open the shoulder and ensure full overhead extension. We start this movement in rack position and rotate to a pinky-forward position at the top. This can be done with one or two kettlebells, though the 1-arm version is simpler, and requires a bit less shoulder mobility. The same posture and breathing rules apply as they do for the standard barbell press as described above.

It is useful for both strength and the health of the shoulder to keep the shoulder blade "packed" by engaging the lats and pulling down and back as you press the weight up.

KB Military Press
Start

KB Military Press
Finish

KB Military Press
Finish

2 KB Military Press
Start

2 KB Military Press
Finish

PUSH PRESS

The push press can be seen as a regression to the military press. Where in the military press described above, the push press brings in an element of power from the hips. For many this is a more natural movement and most athletes can push press about ⅓ more weight than they can press without the hip drive.

From the press start position - weight racked at the shoulder - hinge back at the hips and bend the knees slightly, as if getting ready to jump. The torso should remain upright. Explosively return to the standing position and press the weights overhead at the same time. It is critical that you keep the heels planted at all times. This is hard to do, and it is where most people mess up the exercise...but we really don't want to be up on our tiptoes when balancing weight overhead. You can practice this by doing the lift with the toes intentionally held off the ground.

Return the load to the shoulder, and catch the weight with another slight hip dip to cushion the load.

KB Military Push Press
Start

KB Military Push Press
Dip

KB Military Push Press
Top

KB Military Push Press
Top

KB Military Push Press
Dip

KB Military Push Press
Finish

| 2 KB Military Push Press Start | 2 KB Military Push Press Dip | 2 KB Military Push Press Top |

THE PULL

There is no arguing that pulling is what we do when we climb. It follows that most climbers' additional training includes even more pulling than they do on the rock, and lots of it. Over the years, we have seen more and more problems arise from pulling too much - shoulder and neck pain, bad elbows, and overtraining. For the most part, climbers test out in the elite levels of pulling strength (versus normal populations), and very likely don't need a whole lot more of it.

Our programs are aimed at balancing pulling strength, addressing horizontal versus vertical pulling, and learning more difficult or more complex versions of the exercises in order to focus our climbers' efforts on intensity rather than volume.

PULL-UP

The pull-up is one of the classic upper body strength exercises. It is a landmark strength movement. Although highly bastardized into lesser versions, the strict pull-up is a great movement.

Start with the hands shoulder-width apart on an overhead bar, with elbows locked straight and shoulders in the "packed" position.

In a smooth, SLOW movement, pull until your entire head is above the bar or until the bar touches the collarbones. The top of the range is the hardest, and thus should be the focus of your practice as you work toward your first full pull-up. Reverse the movement exactly: slow, controlled, and ending in the straight elbow, packed shoulder position. Regressions include (in order): 3 second lock off at top, 3 second negative, 1/4 chin up from top, 1/2 chin up from top, 3/4 chin up from top, and full chin. Progressions include tactical pull-up, L-pull-up, weighted pull-up, and offset variations.

REGRESSIONS AND PROGRESSIONS:

3 SECOND HANG, TOP POSITION, REVERSE GRIP

Step up to the bar on a box or chair, then slowly pick your feet up and hold for a full one second. Advance to three, then five seconds before moving to negatives.

3sec hang, top position, reverse grip

3 SECOND NEGATIVE, REVERSE GRIP

From a top starting position, lower slowly and evenly through the full range of motion.

3sec negative, reverse grip

¼ CHIN

From the top start position and using a reverse grip, lower ¼ of the way to the bottom, and pull yourself back up.

¼ Chin-Up Position

½ CHIN

From the top start position and using a reverse grip, lower 1/2 way to the bottom (elbow to 90 degrees), and pull yourself back up.

½ Chin-Up Position

¾ CHIN

From the top start position and using a reverse grip, lower 3/4 of the way to the bottom, and pull yourself back up.

¾ Chin-Up Position

CHIN-UP

Full range of motion. Starting at bottom position and using a reverse grip, chin until neck touches the bar, then lower back down under control until elbows are locked.

Full Chin-Up Position

PULL-UP

With a hands-forward grip, pull through a full range of motion, elbows straight to neck touching the bar.

Pull-Up
Start

Pull-Up
Top

TACTICAL PULL-UP

Set up as for the normal pull-up, but with thumbs on the same side of the bar as fingers. Place the body into the "hollow position," just as you would in the hardstyle plank or in setting up for an ab wheel roll out. Pull to the top position (neck to bar), pause 1 second at top, then lower to the bottom. Pause 1 second at the bottom, then repeat.

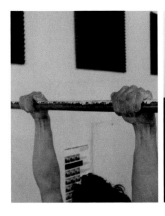

| Tactical Pull-Up Grip | Tactical Pull-Up Start | Tactical Pull-Up Top |

WEIGHTED PULL-UPS

Use a tight-fitting belt (not a dip belt - a harness waistbelt is best) and be a total stickler for ROM. Progressions beyond 5 reps are not necessary. The closer you can snug the weight to the hips, the better. A dangling weight tends to make you swing around a bit.

| Weighted Pull-Up Start | Weighted Pull-Up Halfway | Weight Pull-Up Top |

PULL-UP, ONE HAND ON TOWEL

Use a hand towel (gym rag). Place one hand over the bar, the other will hold on to a towel that has been folded over the bar. Follow the same range of motion rules as a normal pull-up. Start with the "strong hand" on the bar for specified reps, rest briefly (10-15 sec), then repeat with the "stronger hand".

To really progress your pull strength, you need to focus on two things: perfect form and high volume. Work on avoiding failure, rather stop at about half the reps of which you think you're capable. This way you can get twice as many fresh reps per session or per day.

Ladders effectively manage fatigue by keeping the reps very low on most of the sets. If you can do five reps of a particular variation of the pull-up, you could effectively train ladders of 1,2,3 reps repeatedly in a session. Instead of eeking out 3 sets of 5 (15 reps), you might do 3 ladders of 1,2,3 for 18 reps, seeing higher levels of strength for each pull.

Pull-Up	Pull-Up	Pull-Up
One Hand on Towel	One Hand on Towel	One Hand on Towel
Start	Halfway	Top

L-PULL-UP

To perform the L-Pull-Up, start in the same position you would for a standard pull, but then move the legs into the "L" position, with the hips hinged to 90 degrees and the knees locked straight. The real chore is to hold this position for the whole rep.

L-Pull-Up
Start

L-Pull-Up
Top

ROW

We train the rowing movement (horizontal pull) either by suspending the body or by lifting a weight. Our favorite variants are the inverted row and the dumbbell row, detailed below.

INVERTED ROW

The inverted row should be a part of any upper body program. It is an excellent horizontal pull movement that has the added benefit of integrating core stability into the move. You can use any of several implements, but our favorite is a suspension trainer (TRX) or set of rings. Begin with straight arms in a rigid position, effectively the opposite of the way you'd set up for the push-up. From the bottom lock into a "proud chest", squeeze the lats, and pull to a locked position with the hands at the sides of the ribs. Hold the wrists neutral at all times. If you can't do the full range of motion, change your foot position to place the feet further under the body until you are in a position where the move is smooth and complete. You can also do this movement on a fixed bar or even on an Olympic bar in a power rack.

| TRX Inverted Row Start | TRX Inverted Row Halfway | TRX Inverted Row Top |

SINGLE-ARM INVERTED ROW

This exercise is set up the same as the standard inverted row, except that the plan is to do the movement with just one arm. Naturally, the loading of the arm is increased, but the real value in this exercise is the core tension required to do it correctly. You'll set up with a ring or TRX and hold onto it with both hands. Place the feet just slightly wider than shoulder-width apart, then release one of the hands. Keeping the shoulders square, pull until the handle reaches the side of the ribcage, then slowly return to the start position. You can also do this movement on a fixed bar or even on an Olympic bar in a power rack.

Single-Arm Inverted Row Start   Single-Arm Inverted Row Halfway   Single-Arm Inverted Row Top

SINGLE-ARM INVERTED ROW WITH ROTATION

The single-arm inverted row with rotation is potentially the most sport-specific pulling exercise for climbing. The set-up is the same as the normal inverted row, except when you release the non-working arm at the start, you'll allow your body to rotate away from the handle, with your non-working side drifting toward the floor. When fully progressed, your torso should be almost perpendicular to the floor at the bottom of the movement. To start the movement, rotate back to parallel while pulling with the working arm. Continue the rotation, and reach up along the TRX strap (or past the bar) as you lock off. At the top, you should be almost fully rotated toward the working arm.

You'll have a natural rotation at the hips and knees as you do this. However, it is useful to get in the habit of keeping the feet planted in the same spot to avoid having to adjust your stance with each rep.

Single-Arm Inverted Row
With Rotation
Start

Single-Arm Inverted Row
With Rotation
Halfway

Single-Arm Inverted Row
With Rotation
Top

SINGLE-ARM DUMBBELL ROW

This exercise is the workhorse horizontal pull exercise in a weight room. It can be a very basic, lightweight rehab movement and can be a heavy power movement, as well. The setup is to use a flat bench, with one hand and the same-side knee placed on the bench. With the opposite hand, you hold a dumbbell straight down at arm's length. Under control and without rolling the shoulder, pull the dumbbell to the side of the ribs, then return it to the start position. Keep the elbow close to the ribs as you pull, and hold the shoulders square. If it looks like you are starting your lawn mower, it's too heavy. Start with your non-dominant side, then follow with the stronger side.

DB Row	DB Row	DB Row
Start	Halfway	Top

THE CORE

We consider the core everything between the shoulders and the knees, and regard it more as a base of stability than anything else. The core is where we either transfer or lose power in every movement.

CORE TRAINING IS NOT GOING TO GET RID OF FAT ON YOUR BELLY. By now you should know this, but for those who have not been keeping up, we'll explain. The abdominals, obliques, and transversus are the primary groups that most of us try to target when doing ab exercises. These are important muscles to strengthen, but exercising them to reduce the fat that happens to lay on top of them is futile. Once again, I'll reference the University of Virginia study that showed you'd have to do 700 crunches each day for a year to burn a pound of fat. Since spot reduction has been proven over and over again to be ineffective, even doing those 365 workouts might not give you the desired results. If your belly fat is bugging you, it's time to step away from the donut box and buy some spinach.

CORE TRAINING IS NOT "BACK STRENGTHENING." Strong abs do not mean a strong low back. The exercises described here are safe for the low back if done properly, but should not be seen as a direct way to make the back stronger. A huge misconception for sufferers of low back pain is the idea that spinal flexion exercises, such as the abdominal crunch, are good for the back. In fact, it has been shown that repeated spinal flexion is overwhelmingly a bad idea if you have back pain. Dr. Stuart McGill has several excellent books on low back disorders and injuries, and if you have back problems we recommend picking up Back Mechanic.

THE CORE SHOULD NOT BE TREATED AS A PRIME-MOVER. There are many exercises that target the abdominals, but the abs should be trained the way they are used- as structural support. Most of the ab exercises we learned as young athletes use the rectus abdominus to create either hip flexion (as in supine leg raises) or trunk flexion (as in crunches or sit-ups). Although these do "work" the abs, that's not how we use the muscles in normal movement. The core muscles are almost exclusively stabilizers, and are best used to control movement rather than to initiate it. The one exception which may be specific to climbing is the hanging leg raise and its variations.

IT'S MORE THAN ABS. The core, or what we prefer to call the midsection, includes all of the muscles that connect to your pelvis and low back.

> The rectus abdominis
> The transversus abdominis
> The internal and external obliques
> All hip extensors (glutes, hamstrings, etc.)
> The hip flexors

The spine extensors (spinal erectors, quadratus lumborum)
The hip adductors and abductors
The latissimus dorsi

We want to be strong, so clearly, crunches won't do the trick. We are looking for high-load, integrative exercise that will actually change the way your core functions in climbing. Being able to crank out five more reps of a rectus abdominis-focused exercise won't do it.

Although the core can be trained any number of ways, there are two big-bang movements that we like to build most of our programs around. One is trunk flexion, best trained with a simple ab wheel. The other is hip flexion, best trained with the leg raise. Below we'll describe both exercises and their progressions and regressions.

TRUNK FLEXION

BALL ROLL-OUT

This regression of the ab wheel exercises is done with a stability ball instead of the wheel. Set up in a plank position with your forearms placed parallel on the ball, and the feet at shoulder width apart. Using your tension techniques from earlier in the book, hold the hips and core stable while slowly rolling the ball away from you. Most people will reach a point where the core is maximally loaded before they reach full extension of the elbow. You should plan to limit the range of motion based on whether you can hold the core stiff throughout the range.

Once you reach the end of the range, return to the start position, slowly and in control. Once you can do 5-8 reps on a 5 second clock, you are probably ready to advance to the partial ab wheel roll-out.

Ball Roll-Out
Start

Ball Roll-Out
Top

AB WHEEL ROLL-OUT

The Ab Wheel Roll-Out is an easy one to mess up, so careful attention to form is critical. The roll-out as performed correctly with the ab wheel is one of the most effective abdominal strength exercises you'll do. Position yourself with knees on a pad, pre-contract the abs so that you move into the "cat" position (drawing ribcage close to the hips), squeeze the glutes tight, then with the wheel on the floor in front of the knees, roll out the end of your comfortable range of motion. Hip angle should be obtuse (not acute) and should remain so throughout the range. A mistake we see with many athletes is to go too far into the movement, and form collapses on the return to the start. Low back pain is a clear indicator you are rolling past your strong range of motion. If you can do more than a few reps, intensify the effort by slowing down.

AB Wheel Roll-Out
Start

AB Wheel Roll-Out
Halfway

AB Wheel Roll-Out
Bottom

PARTIAL AB WHEEL ROLL-OUT

A partial range of motion in the roll-out is a good place to start if you can't quite get the form correct for the whole thing. Your set-up should be the same as the full roll-out, knees on a pad, hands on the wheel and shoulders "locked-in" to position. Flex the glutes and quads and try to get the hips as straight as possible before rolling forward. This is done by accentuating the "cat" position at the top of the move, then maintaining that high level of tension in the abs as you roll forward.

Start with a range of about 12 inches. If your form is perfect, try for 16, then 20, and so on. A chalk mark or small piece of tape on the floor is useful for marking your intended range of motion. Most athletes can progress by 4 or more inches per week, and thus can advance to the standard roll-out in a few weeks' time.

AB WHEEL ROLL-OUT, PAUSING

This variant of the roll-out is a slightly more advanced version of the movement. Set-up exactly as you do the standard exercise, but at the far end of the range, pause for two to five seconds. If you notice any change in form moving back to the start position, your pause is too long. If you can maintain tension at the far end of the range and can return with the same good form, this is an appropriate progression. Once you can do 8 reps with a 5 second pause, you are probably ready to advance to starting on the feet rather than the knees.

AB WHEEL ROLL-OUT, ON FEET

This is a highly stressful version of the movement and should be used only by athletes with a lot of experience at the less-intense versions of the roll-out. This variation starts with the feet placed at shoulder width, and the body rolled forward so the ab wheel can be placed on the floor in front of the feet.

Try to keep the legs as straight as possible to start, and then begin the movement with the same cues you'd use when working from the knees: Tight glutes, tight quads, "cat" position at the shoulders, and high-tension in the abs. It is an excellent idea to start with partial movements, much as we noted above. Start with maybe 12-16 inches of range, and move out only as far as you can maintain strict positioning. A very strong athlete will eventually be able to take this movement all the way to the floor and back up.

AB Wheel Roll-Out
On Feet
Start

AB Wheel Roll-Out
On Feet
Halfway

AB Wheel Roll-Out
On Feet
Bottom

HIP FLEXION

The leg raise is not only the easiest hip flexion exercise to implement, it is quite sport-specific to movements we do every day in climbing. We don't need to underscore the need for this type of strength, so we'll simply get to describing the exercises and how we progress them.

SEATED STRAIGHT LEG RAISE

The seated straight leg raise is a deceptively hard version of the movement, but is a good place to start. Sit in a doorway or between the uprights of a squat rack. Brace yourself in the position with your hands on the uprights or, ideally, by placing a PVC pipe horizontally across the rack. Holding the hands above the head, stack the shoulders above the hips and maintain an upright position. With legs locked straight, pick the heels up off the ground. Avoid leaning back, and accept that a few inches of range might be all you get.

This movement mimics the harder top half of a traditional hanging position raise, and forces the abs to work from a very short position. We like athletes to be strong here (and address any hamstring flexibility issues) before working too deep into the hanging versions of the exercise.

Seated Straight Leg Raise
Start

Seated Straight Leg Raise
Finish

HANGING KNEE RAISE

The hanging knee raise is the simplest of the hanging hip flexion exercises. It is performed on an overhead bar or hangboard that allows for full extension without having the feet touch the ground. From the straight-leg position, bend at the hips and knees, and pull the thighs to a horizontal or slightly higher position. Knees should be bent to 90 degrees at the top of the range. Return to the bottom under control. Once you can do 5-8 reps of this exercise, progress to the Hanging Straight Leg Raise.

Hanging Knee Raise Start Hanging Knee Raise Halfway Hanging Knee Raise Finish

HANGING STRAIGHT LEG RAISE

The hanging straight leg raise is done holding a pull-up bar or hangboard with a supine grip. From a dead stop, bend at the hip, raising the legs straight out in front of you. Keep the knees locked. Once you reach 90 degrees at the hip (legs horizontal) return to the start position with slow control. Failure to complete the full range of motion is indicative of weak core muscles or a lack of hamstring flexibility.

Hanging Straight Leg Raises
Start

Hanging Straight Leg Raises
Finish

KNEES-TO-ELBOWS

This exercise is started in the same position as the Hanging Straight Leg Raise. Instead of simply raising the knees, keep the arms straight and engage the whole torso to lift the knees all the way to touch the elbows. If you need to bend your arms, it indicates a weak upper abdominal. If you can only do "knees to armpits" you probably have a weak integration between shoulders (via the lats) and abs.

Knees-to-Elbow
Start

Knees-to-Elbow
Halfway

Knees-to-Elbow
Finish

ANKLES TO BAR

Ankles to bar is sometimes seen as a progression of the popular knees-to-elbows exercise, but where knees-to-elbows sees the athlete articulate primarily at the shoulder, ankles to bar is a hip flexion movement. For this exercise, you start in the same deadhanging position as the start of the hanging straight leg raise. You'll do the same pull from the bottom as the leg raise, but then simply continue the range to where the toes or ankles touch the bar between your hands.

Hamstring flexibility is as big a limiter as abdominal strength, so many athletes will find themselves bending the knees at the top of the range. Work toward eliminating this bend by stretching the hamstrings between sets and staying very disciplined on each rep.

Ankles to Bar
Start

Ankles to Bar
Halfway

Ankles to Bar
Finish

PHOTO: MEI RATZ

Mobility is a joint's ability to move through its full range-of-motion. It requires correct muscle action on one side of the joint and flexibility on the opposite side to be considered full mobility. An athlete can exhibit excellent flexibility - a great range of motion in muscles and joints - without really having good mobility. Mobility, as defined by sports science, requires control at the end of the range of motion.

Our drills consist of flexibility, mobility, stability, or a combination of the three. Flexibility is a quality associated with muscle, and normally involves passively taking the joint to the limits of its range of motion. As stated above, mobility is the ability to use the joint throughout its intended range of motion. Stability is simply being able to maintain your intended position under load. Although all three are important for athletic development, mobility forms the basis for good movement, and both good flexibility and good stability are build on a base of good mobility.

Most people don't lack mobility or flexibility in the elbows or knees. These are simple joints and maintaining ROM is fairly easy. Where adults tend to start lacking in their ability to move well is in the shoulders and hips. These are multi-directional joints with a lot of muscle groups acting on them. Although we occasionally seem limitations in the wrists, ankles, and neck, our primary focus will be on the shoulders and hips.

SHOULDER MOBILITY

When we do a climbing assessment, each athlete is run through a battery of sport-specific strength tests, energy system tests, and each answers simple questions in order to gauge where they can most improve their climbing. Before any of this happens, though, we test mobility: the ability of the athlete to use the shoulder and hip joints in a fully functional range of motion. If an athlete comes up short on either of these assessments, they get probably the simplest training prescription we can give: Keep doing what you're doing, but add mobility training to your program.

If the climber fails the hip mobility drills, he risks not being able to position his body correctly in strength exercises, but more importantly on the rock. Keeping the body's center of mass correctly positioned is so important that we think hip flexibility and mobility is a better predictor of performance than grip strength. It's the reason that (grudgingly) we, ourselves, train hip mobility every single training session.

Shoulder mobility problems are a great predictor of future shoulder injuries. Performance-wise, we see many climbers (usually male) that can't get their arms straight overhead. The well-developed muscles of the back and the tight muscles of the chest keep those arms locked in the power position, which is hard to break out of. Imagine being so tight in the lats that your reach is effectively reduced by two to three inches. It sounds crazy, but we see it in about a third of the climbers we test.

For a good visual, get somebody to take a picture of you from the side: arms straight up, core tight, no arch in the low back. Are your arms aligned with your spine? Do they line up behind the ear? Can you keep your elbow straight in the top position?

Bad Shoulder Mobility vs. Good Shoulder Mobility

A very simple test of shoulder mobility requires just a ruler or tape measure and goes as follows:

1. Measure the distance from the tip of your middle finger to the distal crease at your wrist (the wrinkle in your skin where your forearm meets your palm). Note this distance.

2. Make a fist in each hand, with the thumb held inside the fingers.

3. Reach behind the back with the left hand over the top and the right hand reaching from below. Have a friend measure the distance between the two.

4. Repeat the same measurement the other way.

5. Compare the two. If the distance is greater than the measurement you got in step one, you might have a shoulder mobility issue that will prevent you from effectively training the shoulder. In general, if an athlete tests more than an inch worse than their hand length, we recommend limited overhead training until mobility improves.

If there is a 25% or more difference left to right, we suggest a visit to a physical therapist. This difference is usually attributable to a shoulder trauma, overuse on one side, or another disorder than might eventually turn into a chronic injury.

If shoulder mobility is looking like a problem, there's no need to freak out and start taking yoga classes. All you need to do is simply add shoulder mobility and stability drills to your current plan. A great time to do these is within the session, between boulder problems or strength exercises...you know, when you normally are chatting or flipping through old issues of Urban Climber. Lack of mobility or the presence of an injury is not a free pass to get out of strength training...just work around it until it improves.

Our go-to shoulder mobility drill is the kettlebell arm bar. We also like to use PVC pipes and elastic bands for some positions. What works best for each athlete is up to individual preference and need. The exercises are below.

ARM BAR

The Arm Bar is a full-value shoulder mobility and stability drill. This is an excellent drill for developing thoracic mobility and shoulder girdle stability. Pick up a light kettlebell and set-up as you would for the Turkish get-up (kettlebell at full extension in the right hand, right knee bent and foot placed on the floor). Stretch the left arm overhead (as opposed to having it out to the side as you would the Turkish get-up, and using the left arm and leg as an axis, bring your right knee up toward the chest and roll to the left. Roll over to bring your chest toward the ground, resting the head on the left biceps or on the ground. Straighten the right leg, and try to push the right hip toward the ground. Creep the left hand "back" left along the floor, and keep both shoulders pulled down and away from the ears. Hold or pulse the position for 30-60 seconds.

Keep in mind that when you start this it will feel hard. Go light on the weight because your loaded shoulder will be firing like crazy. Don't rush driving the hip into the ground too soon...be patient with the exercise.

| Arm Bar Fetal Pos. Start | Arm Bar Fetal Pos. Roll Over | Arm Bar Fetal Pos. Finish |

| Arm Bar Start | Arm Bar Roll Over Pos. 1 | Arm Bar Roll Over Pos. 2 |

| Arm Bar Roll Over Pos. 3 | Arm Bar Roll Over Pos. 4 | Arm Bar Roll Over Pos. 5 |

SUPERBAND SHOULDER MOBILITY

Overhead Latissimus Stretch - Using a resistance band of your choice: Typically the one inch bands provide enough resistance and comfort. Attach the band to a pull-up bar on anything sturdy up overhead. Place your elbow in the loop hanging down. Lean forward, keep your elbow close to your body and stagger your stance to protect the lower back. Continue to lean into the stretch and try to relax the shoulder and keep from resisting the deep stretch. It doesn't matter which leg is staggered forward, we simply do this to protect the low back.

Superband Lat. Stretch
Start

Superband Lat. Stretch
Finish

Shoulder Traction - With a band securely attached to a bar, this time you'll place your hand in the loop. The band should be around your wrist and hooked onto the bottom meat of your hand. If you simply grasp the loop and hold on it will be hard to relax into the stretch because of the tension required to hold on. With the loop around your wrist walk backwards until you have your desired resistance. Hinge at the hip and sink into the stretch. To get into different "corners" of your shoulder, externally and internally rotate your arm. Stop at any areas that feel like they need more stretch.

Superband
Hand Pos. 1

Superband
Hand Pos. 2

| Superband Hand Pos. 3 | Superband Hand Pos. 4 | Superband Lat. Traction |

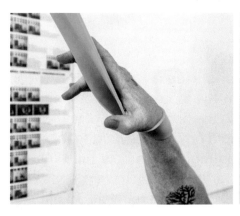

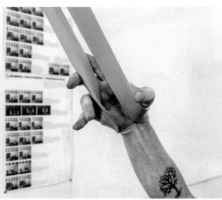

| Superband External 1 | Superband Internal 1 |

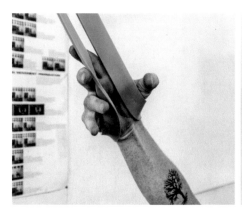

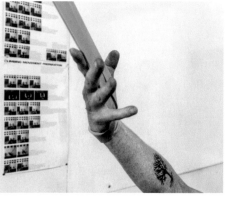

| Superband Internal 2 | Superband Internal 3 |

OVERHEAD SQUAT WITH A PVC PIPE OR DOWEL

Holding a PVC pipe or dowel overhead (hands slightly wider than shoulder width), lock the elbows and lower into a full-depth squat. As your torso leans forward into the movement, the overhead position will naturally stretch the pecs and lats. Try to keep the arms aimed straight at the ceiling, and move the hands as far apart as needed to keep the elbows straight and the bar straight above the feet. If you start to have too much forward lean before the bottom of the squat, simply stop at that point and work from there until your range improves.

Although we classify this as a shoulder mobilizer, it is also a good opportunity to work on your squat mobility, too.

PVC Overhead Squat
Start

PVC Overhead Squat
Start

PVC Overhead Squat
Halfway

PVC Overhead Squat
Halfway

PVC Overhead Squat
Bottom

PVC Overhead Squat
Bottom

HIP MOBILITY

If you want to see the damage that a desk job can do, teach squats to a group of adults. Many of us spend our days sitting at a desk, drive in a car for an hour or more, sit on the couch for a couple of hours, then curl up in bed...with our hips at basically the same angle. Those of us that are active might throw in an hour of weights or time in the rock gym, but it's hardly enough to balance the time spent in the seated position. As we sit, our hip flexors (primarily the iliacus and psoas major) are held in a shortened position, while the hip extensors (glutes in this case) are held in an artificially lengthened position.

Over time, this position becomes "normal" for our hips, and we begin to hold a similar position even while standing, relying not on our bones to maintain erect posture, but the muscles of the back.

Postural problems aside, a lack of hip mobility creates problems for the athlete. Like the group of adults mentioned above, most of us are unable to do a normal range of motion squat once we pass adolescence. This is a fundamental human movement, and being able to effectively use that range is critical to success in climbing. The deep squat pattern isn't the only one we're talking about, either. We also need "turnout", we need the ability to high step both inside (in front of the body) and outside (to the side of the body), and we need to be able to fully extend, such as in long reaches.

Just like shoulder mobility, hip mobility needs to take a priority spot in your training. Treating this training just like any other exercise is the only way to see forward progress. Yes, you can dedicate whole sessions to it. Yes, you can take Yoga classes. But in our experience, people who are willing to dedicate time to Yoga aren't the ones who need help...it's rare for a very immobile person to take up a passion for mobility, much as it's rare for a fearful climber to suddenly take up headpointing on grit. For most of us, the mobility work needs to "sneak" into the program.

We suggest doing mobility as a "third" exercise in a group that includes a big primary movement and a supplemental movement. For example, you could do a set of 3 heavy deadlifts, 5 front levers, and a hip mobility drill. Over the course of one workout, the mobility serves as active rest, and will get trained for several minutes each day...all without feeling like you're "wasting time" doing it. If we asked you to do 10 minutes of hip mobility at the end of a session...you'd have somewhere you needed to be instead. You can also hit the hip mobility drills in the midst of a bouldering or route session. We suggest doing a couple of problems, then a hip mobility drill, a couple more problems, then shoulders, etc.

The basic prescription is to do mobility one day per week for each decade of your life. You're in your thirties - do three days of mobility. In your fifties, do 5. By doing several one-minute sets of mobility drills within the framework of your normal training, this is pretty easy to fit in, and will pay off big dividends in the end.

FROG STRETCH (AND VARIATIONS)

The frog drill is a hip-opener that will help not only with improving your squat form, but with your turn-out on the rock. The frog is performed prone, with the knees turned out to the sides, and placed on a mat. Most knees can't handle this exercise on a hard floor. Turn the feet out to the sides, and place the elbows on the ground directly below the shoulders, most of your weight should be on your arms. Rock the hips back toward the heels, then move them slowly up toward the elbows. Once at the top position, try to move the knees out to the sides slightly, then repeat the motion.

Frog Stretch
Start

Frog Stretch
Finish

SIDE SPLIT VARIATION

To perform the Side Split Variation, from the top frog position, lean to one side and slide the other leg out to a straight position directly to the side. Sag back for a stretch of the hamstring. Hold for 20-30 seconds, then repeat on the other side. Move slowly into this position and work on pivoting off the heel to get into different parts of the stretch.

Frog Stretch
Split Variation

Frog Stretch
Split Variation

DROP KNEE VARIATION

To perform the Drop Knee Variation, rotate one leg internally with the knee planted on the floor until the hip touches the floor. The foot will raise in the air, and will end up slightly to the outside of the knee at the end of the range of motion. Do 3-5 reps per side, resetting the frog with each repetition.

Frog Stretch
Drop Knee Variation

TUG OF WAR SQUAT

The tug of war squat can be seen as a standing frog stretch. Holding onto a solid object, such as the upright on a power rack or a door frame, squat down to below parallel. Once in the bottom position, drive the heels into the floor, hold the torso upright, and gently rock back and forth to relax into the hip stretch. Use this to practice the perfect bottom position in the squat.

Tug of War Squat
Start

Tug of War Squat
Bottom

KNEELING HIP FLEXOR

The kneeling hip flexor stretch is a staple in our exercise programs. It's important to treat this as an active stretch of the hip flexor instead of a passive stretch of the quadriceps. To perform this movement, assume a half-kneeling position. The front calf should be close to vertical, and the rear thigh should be, as well. Be sure to point the rear foot backward - don't plant the toes. Assume a tall-spine position, and look straight forward.

Place the hands on the hips. Flexing the rear hamstring and glute, try to "tip" the hips backward. It is useful to imagine the hips as a large bowl of water and you're trying to pour the water down the back of your leg. By actively contracting the glute, we can get a good stretch in the hip flexor. The active flexing of the muscles on the rear of the leg will inhibit tension in the flexors, and allow for a better stretch than if you just leaned back into the muscle.

Once you have fully contracted the glutes and are pulled up with a tall spine, you can gently drift the hips forward. Remember that this is not a quad stretch - you should be looking for a stretch in the top of the hip - so don't drift too far forward into a "Three Musketeers" stance. You may still feel a stretch in the front of the thigh, but it's not the only stretch you are looking for. Pulse in and out of the stretch 3-5 times per side.

Kneeling Hip Flexor
Start

Kneeling Hip Flexor
Flexed

CHAPTER 13

STRENGTH TRAINING PLANS

PHOTO: MEI RATZ

The following plans cover a wide variety of schedules, tools, and volume. Although we try to lay out as much information on varying these plans as possible, every athlete needs to take personal responsibility to tailor training to their own schedule and level of fitness. You will have questions, but those questions are often best answered by simply looking at your plan and your behaviors, rather than seeking out specific prescriptions from another person.

All climbers are capable of increasing their fitness. We encourage you to understand that there are no quick fixes in strength training, and that the reason most programs are 4 or 8 or 12 weeks is because that is how long it takes for your body to adapt. Some of us, notably older athletes, females, and elites, will take longer to see gains in strength on almost every program. Therefore, it may be wise to plan a couple of extra weeks on any given cycle.

It cannot be overstated that *training works*. If you are not getting stronger, if your numbers are not improving, then you need to go back and assess your plan. Am I doing the appropriate volume? Am I adding too much "extra" stuff to the training? Am I working at heavy enough loads? Once you see good gains for a few weeks and those gains start to go flat, then it is time to make adjustments. Vary your exercises, your schedule, or your training days, or make the leap to another plan.

Although our plans frequently overlap between the climbing gym, hangboard, and weight room, we categorize them in the following section into three broad areas:

Resistance Training Plans - These are total-body strength plans, with most sessions featuring general strength exercises in the weight room.

Finger Strength Plans - These are finger and grip strength plans that can usually be done with just a hangboard or a loading block.

Integrated Strength Plans - These plans feature combination sessions that include finger strength and general strength in the same training session.

RESISTANCE TRAINING PLANS

INTRODUCTION TO STRENGTH PLAN

This program is designed for climbers who have been actively climbing in the gym or outside and are considering adding structured training to their program. This plan features fundamental strength exercises and hangboard work. This is designed to be added to a 2-3 day per week climbing schedule. Time commitment is two sessions per week, with 2-3 hours per week total training time.

For the most part, your climbing plan will remain unaffected. However, we will make some recommendations on session length and scheduling. The schedule for weeks 1, 2, and 4 are the same. Week 3 features three strength and hangboard sessions, and is the most intense of the cycle.

This is a detailed introduction to training. You can change the specific days you train, but if you are new to exercise or to resistance training, know that the sessions and rest days are sequenced and paced out in this way on purpose. If you modify the plan by too much, your results will be compromised.

	M	TU	W	TH	F	SA	SU
WEEK 1	Strength Training + Hangboard	Climbing	Rest	Strength Training + Hangboard	Rest	Climbing - High Volume	Climbing- Easy
WEEK 2	Strength Training + Hangboard	Climbing	Rest	Strength Training + Hangboard	Rest	Climbing - High Volume	Climbing- Easy
WEEK 3	Strength Training + Hangboard	Rest	Strength Training + Hangboard	Rest	Strength Training + Hangboard	Climbing	Rest
WEEK 4	Strength Training + Hangboard	Climbing	Rest	Strength Training + Hangboard	Rest	Climbing- High Volume	Climbing- Easy

TRAINING DETAIL:

WEEK 1, MONDAY

STRENGTH TRAINING

This session is designed to help you improve the strength that matters most for climbing: upper body pulling, core tension, and single leg strength. If you are familiar with weight training exercises, most of what you see here will be very familiar. The exercises are grouped into pairs, and you'll complete three sets of each pair before moving onto the next group. Rest 30-60 seconds between exercises, and take 2-3 minutes between groups. Adjust the load or difficulty of the exercises to make sure that you can just barely complete the recommended number of repetitions in the final set. Keep the load the same for all three sets.

Each workout should start with a good, solid movement preparation warm-up that is 8-10 minutes long.

3 SETS EACH
A1: Pull-Ups x5
A2: Walking Lunges x5+5

B1: Dumbbell Row x5+5
B2: Seated Straight Leg Raise x10

C1: Split Squat x5+5
C2: Hardstyle Plank 15sec

HANGBOARD

This hangboard session will feature two different hand positions. You'll complete 6 sets of position 1 before moving on to 6 sets of position 2. Select one large edge and one small one; the small one should be one you can hang for about 10 seconds. Starting with the large edge, hang for 10 seconds, followed by 50 seconds of rest. You'll do this for 6 rounds, or for 6 minutes total. If you complete all the hangs easily this first workout, plan to add 5-10 pounds to a belt in the next session.

Once you have completed the 6 rounds on the large edge, rest 2-3 minutes before moving on to the small one. This edge, you'll hang for just 5 seconds each minute, with 55 seconds rest between. Again, you'll complete 6 rounds. Instead of adding load if you complete all the sets easily, plan to try a slightly smaller hold next workout. Remember that if you add weight to the large edge, it will make next workout's small edge hang harder, so avoid increasing weight and reducing the small edge in the same session.

To recap:

6 ROUNDS
Large Edge 10sec hang, 50sec rest.

Rest 2-3 minutes

6 ROUNDS
Small Edge 5sec hang, 55sec rest.

WEEK 1, TUESDAY

Climbing. Your fingers may be tired from Monday, so start easy and adjust the session based on yesterday's work.

WEEK 1, WEDNESDAY

Rest. Rest means rest. No easy climbing, no "just going for a run." Today your training time can be dedicated to shopping for training food, to preparing meals for the rest of the week, or to stretching and mobility.

WEEK 1, THURSDAY

STRENGTH TRAINING

Based on Monday's loads, you can probably add weight to today's training in most of the exercises. Remember, you want to make sure you can execute the movements perfectly - if adding load changes your form for the worse, back off until you are better at the movements.

Each workout should start with a good, solid movement preparation warm-up that is 8-10 minutes long.

3 SETS EACH
A1: Pull-Ups x5
A2: Walking Lunges x5+5

B1: Dumbbell Row x5+5
B2: Seated Straight Leg Raise x10

C1: Split Squat x5+5
C2: Hardstyle Plank 15sec

HANGBOARD

6 ROUNDS
Large Edge 10sec hang, 50sec rest. Add load over Monday's session if necessary.

Rest 2-3 minutes

6 ROUNDS
Small Edge 5sec hang, 55sec rest. Reduce hold size
if necessary.

WEEK 1, FRIDAY

Rest. Spend your training time today, if you have time planned, walking. You might think it's crazy, but medium-paced walking is excellent for recovery, for keeping your metabolism moving, and for weight control. Walk, don't run.

WEEK 1, SATURDAY

Climb, high volume. Whether you typically boulder or climb routes, today should be looked at as adding 10-20% total work time over your typical session. If you boulder for an hour normally, go an hour and 10 minutes. If you normally climb 10 pitches in the gym, go for 12.

WEEK 1, SUNDAY

Climbing. This should be a normal climbing day. Since tomorrow is another strength day, consider controlling the intensity to allow for recovery before that session.

WEEK 2, MONDAY

STRENGTH TRAINING

Based on last Thursday's loads, you can probably add weight to today's training in most of the exercises. Remember, you want to make sure you can execute the movements perfectly - if adding load changes your form for the worse, back off until you are better at the movements.

Movement Preparation + Warm-Up, 8-10 minutes.

3 SETS EACH
A1: Pull-Ups x5
A2: Walking Lunges x5+5

B1: Dumbbell Row x5+5
B2: Seated Straight Leg Raise x10

C1: Split Squat x5+5
C2: Hardstyle Plank 15sec

HANGBOARD

6 ROUNDS
Large Edge 10sec hang, 50sec rest. Add load over last week's session if necessary.

Rest 2-3 minutes

6 ROUNDS
Small Edge 5sec hang, 55sec rest. Reduce hold size if necessary.

WEEK 2, TUESDAY

Climbing. This is your fourth day on. Adjust the volume and load as needed. Remember, the focus of your training this month is strength, so less-than-perfect climbing is OK.

WEEK 2, WEDNESDAY

Rest. As we said before, it's a good habit to take you training time and dedicate it to meal preparation and mobility training.

WEEK 2, THURSDAY

STRENGTH TRAINING

Based on Monday's loads, you can probably add weight to a couple of exercises.

Movement Preparation + Warm-Up, 8-10 minutes.

3 SETS EACH
A1: Pull-Ups x5
A2: Walking Lunges x5+5

B1: Dumbbell Row x5+5
B2: Seated Straight Leg Raise x10

C1: Split Squat x5+5
C2: Hardstyle Plank 15sec

HANGBOARD

6 ROUNDS
Large Edge 10sec hang, 50sec rest. Add load over Monday's session if necessary.

Rest 2-3 minutes

6 ROUNDS
Small Edge 5sec hang, 55sec rest. Reduce hold size if necessary.

WEEK 2, FRIDAY

Rest.

WEEK 2, SATURDAY

Climb, high volume. Whether you typically boulder or climb routes, today should be looked at as adding 10-20% total work time over your typical session. If you boulder for an hour normally, go an hour and 10 minutes. If you normally climb 10 pitches in the gym, go for 12. This should be roughly the same total volume as your session from last Saturday.

WEEK 2, SUNDAY

Climbing. Today, you'll probably feel stronger and fresher than you did last Sunday. Keep the volume steady, and don't push too hard. Next week gets tough.

WEEK 3, MONDAY

STRENGTH TRAINING

Keep the loads the same as you did last Thursday, but try to get 2-3 more reps in each set than you did last week. Again, stop before your form starts to break down.

Movement Preparation + Warm-Up, 8-10 minutes.

3 SETS EACH
A1: Pull-Ups x8
A2: Walking Lunges x8+8

B1: Dumbbell Row x8+8
B2: Seated Straight Leg Raise x12

C1: Split Squat x8+8
C2: Hardstyle Plank 15sec (do not increase duration,
 increase intensity)

HANGBOARD

On the hangboard, we are going to increase your hang times, but as with the weight training, keep the loads the same as last week.

6 ROUNDS
Large Edge 15sec hang, 45sec rest.

Rest 2-3 minutes

6 ROUNDS
Small Edge 8sec hang, 52sec rest. Reduce hold size
if necessary.

WEEK 3, TUESDAY

Rest. Walk if you need some activity. Nothing else.

WEEK 3, WEDNESDAY

STRENGTH TRAINING

Maintaining the same reps you did on Monday, you might be able to add load to an exercise or two. If not, just work through the same weight.

Movement Preparation + Warm-Up, 8-10 minutes.

3 SETS EACH
A1: Pull-Ups x8
A2: Walking Lunges x8+8

B1: Dumbbell Row x8+8
B2: Seated Straight Leg Raise x12

C1: Split Squat x8+8
C2: Hardstyle Plank 15sec (do not increase duration, increase intensity)

HANGBOARD

Maintain loads and durations from Monday.

6 ROUNDS
Large Edge 15sec hang, 45sec rest.

Rest 2-3 minutes

6 ROUNDS
Small Edge 8sec hang, 52sec rest. Reduce hold size if necessary.

WEEK 3, THURSDAY

Rest.

WEEK 3, FRIDAY

STRENGTH TRAINING

Maintaining the same reps and loads you did on Wednesday.

Movement Preparation + Warm-Up, 8-10 minutes.

3 SETS EACH
A1: Pull-Ups x8
A2: Walking Lunges x8+8

B1: Dumbbell Row x8+8
B2: Seated Straight Leg Raise x12

C1: Split Squat x8+8
C2: Hardstyle Plank 15sec (do not increase duration, increase intensity)

HANGBOARD

Maintain loads and durations from the previous two sessions.

6 ROUNDS
Large Edge 15sec hang, 45sec rest.

Rest 2-3 minutes

6 ROUNDS
Small Edge 8sec hang, 52sec rest. Reduce hold size if necessary.

WEEK 3, SATURDAY

Climbing. Do a normal climbing session, but understand you are probably a little weak from the hard training this week. Don't go too hard today.

WEEK 3, SUNDAY

Rest.

WEEK 4, MONDAY

STRENGTH TRAINING

This workout, you'll keep the same reps as last week, but add load as able.

Movement Preparation + Warm-Up, 8-10 minutes.

3 SETS EACH
A1: Pull-Ups x8
A2: Walking Lunges x8+8

B1: Dumbbell Row x8+8
B2: Seated Straight Leg Raise x12

C1: Split Squat x8+8
C2: Hardstyle Plank 15sec (do not increase duration, increase intensity)

HANGBOARD

Add load or reduce small crimp size if you are feeling especially strong. Otherwise, maintain loads.

6 ROUNDS
Large Edge 15sec hang, 45sec rest.

Rest 2-3 minutes

6 ROUNDS
Small Edge 8sec hang, 52sec rest. Reduce hold size if necessary.

WEEK 4, TUESDAY

Climbing. This should feel like a pretty normal climbing session. Your overall strength is up, so don't be surprised if you start seeing a little better performance.

WEEK 4, WEDNESDAY

Rest. Meal prep and mobility.

WEEK 4, THURSDAY

STRENGTH TRAINING

This is your last strength session of the phase. This workout, you'll keep the same reps as Monday's session, but add load as able.

Movement Preparation + Warm-Up, 8-10 minutes.

3 SETS EACH
A1: Pull-Ups x8
A2: Walking Lunges x8+8

B1: Dumbbell Row x8+8
B2: Seated Straight Leg Raise x12

C1: Split Squat x8+8
C2: Hardstyle Plank 15sec (do not increase duration, increase intensity)

HANGBOARD

Maintain loads from Monday.

6 ROUNDS
Large Edge 15sec hang, 45sec rest.

Rest 2-3 minutes

6 ROUNDS
Small Edge 8sec hang, 52sec rest. Reduce hold size if necessary.

WEEK 4, FRIDAY

Rest.

WEEK 4, SATURDAY

Climb, high volume. This will be your highest-volume day of the phase. Go 10% over your best for the month.

WEEK 4, SUNDAY

Climb easy today. At the end of this phase, take 2-3 days completely off and then start your next 4-week training plan.

THE 40-DAY PLAN, 5X2 AND 2X5

This is our favorite off-season training program. We have both had great success with this plan personally and it has worked well for many of our athletes. It is a low-volume, easy-paced program, but requires 5 days per week in the weight room for short 20 to 50 minute sessions. We first learned about this plan from strength coach Dan John, and have modified it only slightly. As opposed to most of our programs, this is most effectively done for 8 weeks - 40 workouts - which could change the way you look at progress forever.

The general plan is simple. You'll pick five movements, a press, a pull, a hinge, a squat, and a hard core movement. You will do 5 sets of 2 of each exercise on the heavy day, and 2 sets of 5 on the light day. You will alternate between the two days five days per week for 8 weeks. On the far end, you'll be a different athlete. It is not only the simplest way to strength we have found, it is also an exercise in patience, discipline, and faith in the process.

Start with a weight you can handle easily for each exercise. Only go up in load if you are feeling good, and feel free to back off a bit if needed from time to time.

Due to the low volume of the training in this plan, you can successfully combine it with a moderate load finger strength plan. You'll have to work out the details individually, but we recommend a plan such as the Go A Hundred hangboard plan or simple Max Hangs. If you are going to be training for specific climbing strength at the same time as doing the 40-Day Plan, consider selecting a couple of unilateral bodyweight exercises for use in the plan. Instead of bench press or front squats, you might consider the 1-arm push-up and the pistol, both of which will be less exhausting and will leave you with more energy for hard climbing.

An example plan might look like this:

EXERCISE	STARTING LOAD, HEAVY DAY	STARTING LOAD, LIGHT DAY
DEADLIFT	5x2 @ 325	2x5 @ 225
PUSH PRESS	5x2 @ 135	2x5 @ 95
PISTOL SQUAT	5x2 @ 20	2x5 @ B.W.
PULL-UP	5x2 @ 80	2x5 @ 20
ANKLES TO BAR	5x2 Slow	2x5 Fast

This is a good plan to combine with a finger strength program. A good place to start might be to add the Go A Hundred hangboard plan (p. 247) within the circuit on the 5x2 days. Alternatively, you could add a finger strength session at the end of the weight training, maybe 2-3 days per week. As stated elsewhere in this book, it is our belief that finger strength training done in conjunction with weight training will enhance finger strength gains and reduce the chance of injury. It's a win-win, and you'll still have time to get home and help with dinner. Don't overcomplicate it.

BASE STRENGTH

Base means base. This plan is a 4-week repeatable plan that is aimed at climbers who are coming off a layoff or who have not done any strength training before. It is a 3-day per week resistance training plan, with a little bit of climbing sprinkled in. The idea is to build general athleticism - a foundation upon which you can build specific climbing fitness. You can do more climbing than prescribed, but if you are coming off a layoff of more than a couple of months be patient. The longer you take to build up your strength, the longer you'll keep it.

Each of the sessions features five movements, as suggested in the workout templates below. The framework is this:

GROUP A
A1: CORE 1
A2: CORE 2

GROUP B
B1: UPPER BODY PRESS
B2: HIP HINGE

GROUP C
C1: UPPER BODY PULL
C2: SQUAT

The session is set up to do each pair of exercises as a "superset" - doing exercise one followed by exercise two with little rest. After exercise 2, rest 60-90 seconds (longer if needed!), then start in again for the prescribed number of sets.

We suggest exercises for each session below, but you can substitute as necessary. Remember to stick with the same exercises for an entire 4-week cycle, though.

The Rules:

1. Warm up very well. Do a movement preparation sequence and 3-5 minutes of dynamic warm-up. We have found climbing to be a good warm up for these sessions, so if you have access to a gym that features both weights and climbing, you're in luck.

2. Do the exercises right. Strength is a skill, if you're doing the movements wrong, you aren't getting much out of them. Start with the progression or regression where you feel like you have mastered the movement.

3. Never miss a rep. Yes, you want to lift heavy, to the point you almost can't do it. Don't train to failure, though. A good rule of thumb is to stop the set when your movement slows down, even if you haven't completed all the reps.

The plan is fairly simple. We have included suggested climbing here, but don't get too hung up on it. Yes, you can still run or bike or ski at a recreational level...but don't let those activities defocus your strength training.

Strength A + Hangboard	Strength B +45-60 Min. Easy Bouldering	Strength C + Hangboard	Climb Routes or Easy Boulder Problems 60-90 Min.
Strength A + Hangboard	Strength B +45-60 Min. Easy Bouldering	Strength C + Hangboard	Climb Routes or Easy Boulder Problems 60-90 Min.
Strength A + Hangboard	Strength B +45-60 Min. Easy Bouldering	Strength C + Hangboard	Climb Routes or Easy Boulder Problems 60-90 Min.
Strength A + Hangboard	Strength B +45-60 Min. Easy Bouldering	Strength C + Hangboard	Climb Routes or Easy Boulder Problems 60-90 Min.

STRENGTH A (3 SETS OF EACH PAIR)
A1: Ab Wheel Roll-Out x5
A2: Ankles to Bar x5

B1: Push Press x5
B2: Deadlift x5

C1: Pull-Up x5
C2: Goblet Squat x5

STRENGTH B (3 SETS OF EACH PAIR)
A1: Hanging Straight Leg Raise x10
A2: Ab Wheel Roll-Out x5

B1: Overhead 2 Kettlebell Press x5
B2: Kettlebell Swing x20

C1: Inverted Row x5
C2: Walking Lunge x5+5

STRENGTH C (2 SETS OF EACH PAIR)
A1: Knees To Elbows x5
A2: Seated Straight Leg Raise x 10

B1: Push-Up x10
B2: Deadlift x3

C1: Inverted Row x5
C2: Rack Squat x5

The sets should be kept to 3 each for efficiency sake. Reps, we keep in the 5-10 range, which is a bit on the high side for pure strength, but will force you to use slightly lower loads. This lets us train 3 days per week without overtraining.

STRENGTH MAINTENANCE

Strength training is still important, even during your sport specific season. To not strength train in-season, is like putting money away for retirement for eight months out of the year and then proceed to spend part of the money saved the other four months on frivolous items. Why not maintain all your hard work instead of letting it all go just to start over again?

Studies have shown that once you stop training, strength can diminish in as quick as two weeks. If you also stop saving money, you'll save less. You should strength train like you save money. Some months you can sock more away and other months you put just a little away, but at least it's something. How can we stay strong without spoiling game day performance? We will reduce the volume of our strength sessions by two-thirds to one-half, but still lift heavy.

For Example:

Lets say your strength sessions for the deadlift is 225lbs and you did that at 5x2 or 3x3. For in-season training you will perform the same lift at the same weight, but at 3x2, 5x1, or 2x3. Instead of doing 9-10 total reps per workout you're doing 5-6. The volume is lower, but you're still handling the same heavy weight. By doing this you'll never be far from strength. You should perform this 1-2x a week and work it into your training so it doesn't interfere with your scheduled events, most likely a Monday and Wednesday or a Tuesday and Thursday.

Remember to stick with four major movements when strength training.

Hip Hinge - Deadlift or RDL
Squat - Front Squats or 2 Kettlebell Rack Squats
Pull - Pull-ups or some variation of the Row
Push - Push-Up or Military Press

There are lots of options to progress or regress each movement and that's fine, but just stick to the principles. You should pick one of the four patterns to focus on and put the other three in between sets as "fillers," just to grease the groove. Rotate to another movement pattern after 4-6 weeks.

Remember, these session should be approached like you're practicing strength. You are not working hard in these sessions. You are barely breaking a sweat or maybe not sweating at all. At no point are you increasing weight, even if it feels easy. You can attack the numbers once you start your off-season training. Your session should clock in around 30 minutes after you've properly stretched and warmed-up.

Lift heavy weights often. Don't lose what you've already worked so hard to gain.

FINGER STRENGTH PLANS

THE WORLD'S SIMPLEST HANGBOARD SESSION

As if complicating things made them somehow more effective. If you have not been training at all, the most effective solution is to start easy. On the flip-side, if you are bogged down by timing and loading and figuring out optimal hold sizes on the board, you might need to take a step back.

We suggest 8 repeats of this hangboard protocol, with a maximum frequency of 2-3 days per week. It's so short and so simple, you will want to add more to it. We caution you that to do so might diminish the results. Have the courage to focus and you'll be pleased with what you find.

In this session, you're going to pick an edge that you can hang on for 10 to 15 seconds without really fighting. If you've been away for a long time, consider starting this by using a pull-up bar instead of a hangboard. Then, you'll do a simple time ladder:

> Hang for 5 seconds, rest 25
> Hang for 10 seconds, rest 20
> Hang for 15 seconds, rest 15
> This takes 90 seconds. Repeat it four times.

Large Edge

If you complete the whole session without much issue, add 5 pounds for the next session or move to the next-smaller hold, but keep the sets and times fixed.

This session can be done the same day as a weight training session, or the morning before a climbing day.

GO 30

Go 30 is an excellent hangboard plan for 3 different types of climbers:

1. Climbers that are short on time.

2. Climbers that have been away from training for more than 3 months.

3. Climbers that have not trained specific finger strength before.

You will load each position for a total of 30 seconds per session (Go a Hundred, later, is 100 seconds of loading). Hang sets should be between 5 and 20 seconds. At the beginning of each cycle, you'll be using bigger holds and will trend toward the 20 second end of things. As the cycle progresses, you'll be on the smaller holds, and will end up having to do the sets for shorter durations. If you get to where you can't do 5-second hangs, reduce the load.

Select a board with a series of edge sizes. Our preference is a Tension Grindstone Board, but the Eva Lopez boards are good, as would be a well-populated campus board. As opposed to Go a Hundred, we usually just do this plan for one cycle.

Start with the largest edge on the board. On the Grindstone, this will be 35mm, and will be pretty easy for most experienced climbers. This workout should just involve doing 2 sets of 15 second hangs in the half-crimp position or one set of 10 and one set of 20 seconds. Do this for 2 sessions, which can be three days in a row if your schedule allows. Don't add load, just do it at bodyweight, keeping it simple and easy.

Session 3 and 4 you will move to the next smaller edge, which is the 30mm on the Grindstone. This is a bit of a leap, but most climbers will still be able to stick with the 15-20 second sets. Session 5 will see you on the 25mm edge, which you'll do for 2 sessions (sessions 5 and 6). Most climbers spread these sessions out to at least every other day, but we leave this up to the individual.

Sessions 7 and 8 are done on the 20mm edge, then sessions 9 and 10 on the 15mm. Many climbers will be able to stick with 15 or more seconds per hang straight through all 10 sessions. Good job. This is a 10-session cycle, and it doesn't really matter if it takes you 2 weeks or 4 weeks to complete...discipline and patience are the key to getting stronger.

If you need to break these down to 10 second or even 5, that's fine. It just shows us that you'll move through the whole plan more slowly. Here is a review of the progression in table form with some example hold sizes:

SESSION #	EDGE SIZE (HALF CRIMP)	GRINDSTONE	PROGRESSION
1 AND 2	Largest	35mm	Top Edge
3 AND 4	Second-Largest	30mm	24mm
5 AND 6	Mediumest	25mm	20mm
7 AND 8	Second-Smallest	20mm	16mm
9 AND 10	Smallest	15mm	12mm

After you complete all 10 sessions in the series, it is possible to go through and repeat it again at higher loads. However, we suggest that moving up to a higher-volume program is more effective for most climbers. Most times, we suggest the climber move up to a Go 50 plan (50 seconds total hanging) or an intermittent hangs plan.

PHOTO: SAM LIGHTNER, JR.

GO A HUNDRED

Finger strength is indisputably useful in climbing and having more of it usually helps you get better. For many of us, enough finger strength can make up for a lack of technique or power. As much as we'd like to gain this strength quickly, however, it doesn't happen. What's worse...most climbers who have been in the sport for long enough are already close to their genetic potential for strength, so seeing improvements is even harder.

We can't tell you the number of emails we've received about how this or that program didn't work, only to find that the writer of the email didn't really do the complete sessions and didn't follow the program for the whole duration. Of course it didn't work! What is the value of a training program that an athlete can't follow? What is the value of a training program that is so intense that the athlete can't stick with it long enough to get strong?

The major complaint we get about most of our hangboard programs is that they feel too easy. Well, we'd way rather get strong without suffering than suffer without getting strong. That's where this plan really shines - it's simple, progressive, and gets you strong over the long haul.

Go A Hundred is simple. You hang for 100 seconds on an edge, then progress slowly to smaller and smaller holds. This plan is dependent on using a board with multiple hold sizes, such as the Tension Climbing Grindstone Board or the Transgression/Progression Board (assuming you've got thick calluses on your fingertips and a thick wallet in your pocket). It works reasonably well with a campus or system board with multiple edge sizes, but we've found you need about 5 progressively smaller edges to make it work.

Hang sets should be between 5 and 20 seconds. At the beginning of each cycle, you'll be using bigger holds and will trend toward the 20 second end of things. As the cycle progresses, you'll be on the smaller holds, and will end up having to do the sets for shorter durations. If you get to where you can't do 5-second hangs, you're past the point of useful work and increasing your chance of injury...especially at a volume of 100 seconds per session. At this point, you should opt for a bigger series of holds.

Yes, we are aware that a 20 second load edges toward muscular endurance more than strength when it comes to adaptation. We like 20 second loads, though, because we are in a safe zone for the connective tissue in the fingers and because this represents a more real-world load - when we are climbing many of us tend to hang on for longer than 5 seconds per hold. If you think this seems crazy, don't email us about it...just stick with doing repeaters.

The sessions can be done by integrating them with other strength work, or simply as straight sets. Rest as needed. Ahh, yes... "rest as needed." Many people worry "how much time, exactly, should I rest between sets?" It doesn't matter much, but if you're getting pumped as you go through the session, it's not enough rest and if you eat a meal between sets, it might be too much. If you're honestly not sure, go for 3-5 minutes.

The metric should not be how tired the training makes you, but rather how strong.

One recommendation we'll make is to do a quick set of finger extensions (we like the Expand Your Hands Band) for 10 reps per hand. There is good science behind activating antagonists to increase strength in the agonists, but honestly, we just think it makes the fingers feel better!

An Example Session, integrated with weight training:

5 ROUNDS OF
Deadlift x 2
1-Arm 1-Leg Push Up x 2 each side
Pistol Squat x 2 each side
DB Row x 2 each side

Levers x 2
Edge Hang Half Crimp x 20 seconds (or less!)
Extensions x 10 each side

If one didn't get all 100 seconds on the hang, he'd add a few sets at the end. No big deal. Yes, we are only training one hold position. Although we don't feel it's necessary for most climbers, you can add supplemental positions (at significantly reduced volumes). We suggest doing 20-30 seconds of total loading on supplemental positions, in 5-10 second sets. A nice way of setting this up would be to cycle in maybe two other positions in an alternating fashion, like this:

Half Crimp Edge 20 seconds
Hang 2F Pocket 10 sec

Half Crimp Edge 20 seconds
Hang Pinch 10 sec

Half Crimp Edge 20 seconds
Hang 2F Pocket 10 sec

Half Crimp Edge 20 seconds
Hang Pinch 10 sec

Half Crimp Edge 20 seconds
Hang 2F Pocket 10 sec

As always, we'll remind you that the specifics don't matter as much as regular loading and progression through a long cycle. Dialing in some killer session that you only do once or twice in a season is a waste of time. Although it might make you tougher and boost your ego, it won't make you stronger.

CYCLE 1

This is the one you'll feel like you don't need. You're experienced, you just sent 13c, and you've got a "good base" - whatever that means. If you want to get stronger and you want to avoid injury, please don't disregard this cycle. Each time you do this plan, you must do cycle 1 - it's the part that keeps you from getting hurt.

Start with the largest edge on the board. On the Grindstone, this will be 35mm. This workout should just involve doing 5 sets of 20 second hangs. Do this for 2 sessions, which can be three days in a row if your schedule allows. Don't add load, just do it at bodyweight, keeping it simple and easy.

Session 3 and 4 you will move to the next smaller edge, which is the 30mm on the Grindstone. This is a bit of a leap, but most climbers will still be able to stick with the 20 second sets. Session 5 will see you on the 25mm edge, which you'll do for 2 sessions (sessions 5 and 6). Most climbers spread these sessions out to at least every other day, but we leave this up to the individual.

Sessions 7 and 8 are done on the 20mm edge, then sessions 9 and 10 on the 15mm. Many climbers will be able to stick with 20 seconds per hang straight through all 10 sessions. Good job. This is a 10-session cycle, and it doesn't really matter if it takes you 2 weeks or 4 weeks to complete...discipline and patience are the key to getting stronger.

If you need to break these down to 15 second sets, 10 or even 5, that's fine. It just shows us that you'll move through the whole plan more quickly. Here is a review of Cycle 1 in table form with some example hold sizes (same as the Go 30, above):

SESSION #	EDGE SIZE (HALF CRIMP)	GRINDSTONE	PROGRESSION
1 AND 2	Largest	35mm	Top Edge
3 AND 4	Second-Largest	30mm	24mm
5 AND 6	Mediumest	25mm	20mm
7 AND 8	Second-Smallest	20mm	16mm
9 AND 10	Smallest	15mm	12mm

CYCLE 2

After you complete cycle 1, take 3-4 days off from the board. You can climb a little, but remember that the less you stress your fingers, the stronger you'll get in the next cycle. Rest is an integral part of this training. If you made it through the whole progression at 20 seconds per hang, add 20% to your bodyweight for this series. If you dropped down to shorter-duration sets, but were able to stay above the 5 second mark, add 10%. If you were working at 5 second sets by the end, stick with bodyweight.

You will use the exact-same load for the whole cycle, so be conservative.

PERFORMANCE LAST PHASE	LOAD FOR CYCLE 2
All sessions at 20 seconds	Bodyweight + 20%
All sessions at more than 5 seconds	Bodyweight + 10%
Some sessions at 5 seconds	Bodyweight

We are tempted to try to up the ante every time we do well in strength training. In this plan, though, the improvements come by progressing to smaller holds and bringing the loads up slowly. Think long term instead of next week. Think Roth IRA instead of Vegas Strip.

Cycle 2 will feature more rest between sessions. We recommend at least one day between. Again, you can put these in with other strength work, with a mobility session, or even with some bouldering or climbing. Here is a session of integrated strength one of our athletes did recently in cycle 2:

> KB Swing x 10, Overhead Press x 5, Straight Leg Raise x 5, Hang 15mm (+20%) x 15 sec
> KB Swing x 10, Overhead Press x 5, Straight Leg Raise x 5, Hang 15mm (+20%) x 13 sec

KB Swing x 10, Overhead Press x 5, Straight Leg Raise x 5, Hang 15mm (+20%) x 15 sec

Rack Step-Up x 5+5, Pull-Up x 5, Ab Wheel x5, Hang 15mm (+20%) x 12 sec
Rack Step-Up x 5+5, Pull-Up x 5, Ab Wheel x5, Hang 15mm (+20%) x 13 sec
Rack Step-Up x 5+5, Pull-Up x 5, Ab Wheel x5, Hang 15mm (+20%) x 12 sec

TGU x 1+1, Plank Rope Pull x 10m, Frog x 45 sec, Hang 15mm (+20%) x 12 sec
TGU x 1+1, Plank Rope Pull x 10m, Frog x 45 sec, Hang 15mm (+20%) x 8 sec
TGU x 1+1, Plank Rope Pull x 10m, Frog x 45 sec (no hang, 100 sec already done)

You will follow the exact-same progression as Cycle 1. Typically, the first few sessions will go easily, with most hangs at close to 20 seconds. Later in the phase, the sessions can be real grinders. In the latter phases, you may end up with sets of 5-10 seconds, split by lots of rest, for 10-20 sets...a serious day's work.

SESSION #	EDGE SIZE (HALF CRIMP)	GRINDSTONE	PROGRESSION
1 AND 2	Largest	35mm	Top Edge
3 AND 4	Second-Largest	30mm	24mm
5 AND 6	Mediumest	25mm	20mm
7 AND 8	Second-Smallest	20mm	16mm
9 AND 10	Smallest	15mm	12mm

After completing Cycle 2, there are two options. You can once again add 10% or 20% load and complete another training cycle. We recommend this only for athletes that completed Cycle

2 easily, sticking with 10 or more second hangs. If you were getting down into the 5-10 second hang zone, go back to Cycle 1, doing all the hangs at bodyweight for 10 full sessions. This is a finger strength plan that can be done many months per year, and can be "run in the background" with other climbing training, especially during Cycle 1.

7:13 INTERMITTENT HANGS

We have been opposed to time-driven strength sessions for most of our careers. This position is based on the fact that load is the most important factor in gaining strength and taking the time to provide enough load each session is key. This means that worrying about holding rest periods to a specific length should not be important. Several hangboard programs control for both work and rest. Climbers are comfortable with this setup because they don't have to pay attention to what is happening in their muscles - they just respond to the beeping of the alarm.

There is nothing inherently wrong with this type of training. In fact, there are several physiological factors that contribute to good climbing that result from reduced or limited rest, including mental toughness and strength endurance. We still prefer, however, to lean toward creating the maximum strength possible.

Most climbers are familiar with the 7-seconds-on-3-seconds-off cycle of intermittent hangs. It is an effective and popular program. Like every program, however, a climber will see fewer adaptations with each training cycle, to the point that such a program will no longer result in significant gains.

This is exactly where one of the best redpoint climbers in the world was at the end of 2017 when we spoke about hangboarding. He has seriously strong fingers, but had plateaued for the last year or so and was seeking a way forward. A fan of 7:3 hangs, he wanted to know how to manipulate the program he was on in order to start progressing again.

In trying to gain significant strength one of the first places we look is increasing load. Since this climber had probably maxed out what he could do - there is no lack of motivation or toughness here - we next looked at recovery between repetitions. A 7:3 work:rest ratio calls for more than twice as much work as recovery, which is firmly within the realm of hypertrophy and muscular endurance training. In order to keep things simple and maintain the format he liked, we suggested a plan that would reverse the ratio, and we built the 7:13 (approximately a 1:2 work:rest ratio) protocol.

The session called for working three grip positions (edge, pocket, and pinch). Each position was held for 6 repetitions each set, 7 seconds on, 13 seconds off...a total of 2 minutes. This work was followed by a two minute rest. After resting, you'd then repeat the same position for two more full sets. You then follow the same protocol with the pocket and pinch grips. Stick with the same grips for the entire training cycle, and adjust load as needed as you gain strength.

EDGE	POCKET	PINCH
6x7:13 (2:00)	6x7:13 (2:00)	6x7:13 (2:00)
Rest (2:00)	Rest (2:00)	Rest 2:00)
6x7:13 (2:00)	6x7:13 (2:00)	6x7:13 (2:00)
Rest (2:00)	Rest (2:00)	Rest 2:00)
6x7:13 (2:00)	6x7:13 (2:00)	6x7:13 (2:00)
Rest (2:00)	Rest (2:00)	

Most climbers would do a higher-volume session like this in a dedicated strength phase. We suggest doing the sessions 2-3 times per week for most athletes, but aim for the 12 sessions rather than a specific number of weeks. These sessions can be effectively combined with weight lifting sessions or high-intensity core work. Some amount of skill work and easier bouldering can be placed at both ends of the focus session.

PHOTO: NATE LILES

INTEGRATED STRENGTH PLANS

Everything about training for climbing is complicated. It is an exercise in compromise - focus on power and you lose endurance, too much time getting your fingers strong, and your redpoint grade drops. Over the years, there have been many creative solutions proposed to solve this problem. Many programs are more or less stolen from training plans for other sports, which presents a whole host of issues.

The one thing that continues to surface both in the gym and on the rock is that the stronger climbers both avoid injury and send quickly. This is of no surprise: all facets of fitness are derivatives of strength. What is power? Strength times speed. What is endurance? Strength divided by time. The bottom line? The stronger you get, the better everything else gets.

So what's the problem? There's only one, but it's a big one: Strength training takes time, both to execute and to recover from. The recovery is the biggest issue. In fact, people who stall out strength training frequently get everything else right - load, volume, frequency - but they under-recover. Why? Because the overload we experience in strength doesn't "feel" like hard exercise. The sets are short, the cardiovascular component almost nonexistent, and there is never any nausea.

In order to get stronger you need to really overload your system. If you really overload your system you need to rest a lot between efforts. If you rest a lot between efforts, you get bored and start the next set too soon. The solution? Find something productive to do between sets - like mobility.

Heavy strength training and finger strength training are almost an ideal marriage. The high total body loads of the strength sets tend not to affect the finger strength sets and vice versa. However, simply alternating between the two can still result in too little rest.

In order to address this issue, we add much-needed mobility work between these activities, and the result is an ideal mixture of effective training and an efficient use of time.

The Integrated Strength template consists of three exercises done in short "circuit" fashion: a finger strength set, a heavy resistance set, and a mobility exercise. Single circuits take about 5 minutes each. We have found that three rounds of a circuit, about 15 minutes, is the ideal duration of one group. By building three different circuits, you can create an effective and quick training session that clocks in under an hour.

TRAINING: WHERE ARE YOU GOING?

Too often, we are either in the mode of training for something big or doing nothing at all. We ramp it up for a couple of months, send the route, and then hang back and take stock of our achievements. Even worse, sometimes we opt for long-term difficult training programs that look fabulous on paper, but we never seem to execute. But what if there was a better way? What if your underlying goal in training was to develop a readiness for the sport that you could carry with you at all times.

Whether we like it or not, we can only be driving hard part of the time. As the old maxim goes, "If you are always training hard, you're never training hard." A program like the one suggested in this book can deliver is a solid foundation on which to build specific fitness. A two-day per week base of Integrated Strength sessions will marry well with a bouldering phase, a high-volume alpine training phase, or even a peak redpoint phase, all the while allowing you to continually push the juggernaut of strength forward.

There may even be long periods of the year where you do next to nothing on the rock or in the mountains. This minimalist program will keep you fit enough to get back to shape quickly when the opportunity arises. Strength coach Dan John talks about "park bench" and "bus bench" workouts. You're on the bus bench when you are going somewhere, on the park bench when you're not. Integrated Strength makes an excellent holding-pattern session - a park bench workout - when you are not quite ready to lock horns with a project. When it becomes bus bench time, you simply increase your training loads, reduce the hold size on your hangboard sets, and get going.

EXERCISE ONE: FINGER STRENGTH

Most climbers understand that stronger fingers are a benefit in climbing. Simply climbing to gain this strength can result in uneven loading, can allow you to avoid certain difficult hold types, and isn't regular enough an overload to elicit optimum improvement. The tool of the trade is the hangboard. The training for optimum finger strength includes repeated sets of isometric hangs.

We get into trouble when we go too hard or too long on these boards; the very thing that makes you strong so quickly can also injure you. There are several terrible hangboard training programs out there, and there are some very good ones. Even the good ones can lead to trouble, mostly as a result of trying to hurry through the sessions or progress too quickly. A good starting point is to perform 3 sets of 10 seconds in three different hand positions. This workout is so simple and safe that you should stick with it for as long as possible - at the very least ride it out until you no longer see any improvement from it. We will use this set and rep plan in some of the examples below.

When training finger strength, specificity is an important consideration. You want to train both the hold types you use most frequently and the ones that give you the most trouble. A look at any popular hangboard, and you can see that the variety in possible hold combinations is almost endless. Don't get sucked in. There is nothing so special about a particular protocol that makes it "the best"; in fact, the best program is probably to change programs every couple of months! Pick three positions, and train them exclusively through a 4 to 6 week phase. Keep your goal in mind: do you want to be trained or entertained?

EXERCISE TWO: RESISTANCE TRAINING

The stronger you are, the easier everything else in sport becomes. Although for years we insisted that climbing was different from other sports, the fact is that all sports are different from other sports. The common link? The human being. Climbers must generate force the same as everyone else. Yes, we do so by balancing strength with focus, route reading, and fear management, but the mastery of tension forms the base of all we do.

We have to do very sport-specific training, just like every other athlete. But at the core of training, we still find the fundamental human movements. Like it or not, the best way to develop those movements is in non-specific environments. We simply can't generate enough force in climbing specific positions to progress to our full athletic potential.

Although the movements can be divided up a few different ways and can feature subsets, most coaches agree that training the five basic movement patterns give the biggest bang for the buck. Those movements include the Upper Body Press, the Upper Body Pull, the Core, the Hip Hinge, and the Squat.

These patterns are the most useful because they force you to use several muscles at once to produce force. This is both efficient and effective at producing high levels of hormonal activity - which is half the reason we do them.

In this program, we focus on three of the four big movements (Core is added to many sessions but is not a fundamentally taxing pattern). Our movements include the Hip Hinge, Upper Body Press, and Squat. Why no pulling? Well, because you are probably loading the pattern already. More importantly, though, the Hip Hinge is going to be a big pull, and the finger strength sets also represent a pull...enough!

This training plan integrates well with bouldering or route climbing, where you'll be pulling all day long anyway. Remember, the goal of most training is not to improve the things at which you are already elite - it's to shore up the things that are holding you back.

There are many exercises that are appropriate for climbers in each movement pattern, but there are a few that are better than others. The big key is to select exercises that you know, that you can do in your facility, and that you can progress correctly. The patterns and suggested exercises for integrated strength are as follows:

HIP HINGE
Deadlift
Kettlebell Swing
Single-Leg Hip Thrust (bodyweight option)

SQUAT
Pistol Squat
Split Squat
Rack Squat

PRESS
One-Arm Overhead Press
One-Arm Push-Up
Push Press

Full details for these exercises are available in the Exercises section of the book. It is critical to perform the exercises correctly: if you don't know them, don't do them. Find a good strength coach and invest some time and money in learning correct form and loading.

EXERCISE THREE: MOBILITY

Let's review…
Mobility is simply the ability to use a joint through its intended range of motion. For the most part, our knees and elbows aren't

a problem. The shoulders and hips, especially in adults, are an issue. As a general rule, if you can't hold both arms straight above the head without arching your back, your shoulders are too tight. One of the effects of building massive strength and power in the back and shoulders without maintaining mobility is to get tight - so tight that you are effectively shorter when you reach high above your head.

Immobility in the hips is also a problem. If you can't do a full squat with your heels on the ground, or can't get your hips within about 3-4 inches of the ground in a frog stretch, you are probably not going to maximize your body-positioning ability.

The difficulty with mobility work is that it is boring and it's hard to tell if you're getting better. There are two relatively easy tests you can do that will give you a good indication how you are progressing. The first is the hip test mentioned above.

HIP MOBILITY TEST - FROG STRETCH

1. Assume the frog stretch position, with the feet placed against a wall. Your shins should be perpendicular to the wall (right angle at the ankle), and your thighs should be parallel to the wall (right angle at the knee).

2. Bearing most of your weight on the elbows, lean "forward" onto the arms and move the knees as far apart as possible. Realign the legs to get your right angles again if necessary.

3. Once you have relaxed into the stretch, look at how far your hips are from the ground. A good measure is to take a fist and place it on the ground below your pubis - the bottom part of your hip bone that sits right above where you go potty.

4. If your hips touch the fist, your mobility is probably pretty good. More than two fists away from the ground, and you've got some work to do.

SHOULDER MOBILITY TEST

1. Measure the length of your hand from the tip of your middle finger to the distal crease at the junction of your palm and forearm. This is the wrinkle closest to your palm.

2. Next, make two fists, with the thumbs tucked inside. Reach over your head and back with your left hand, and behind your back with the right. Try to get the fists as close as possible together along the spine. Have a partner measure the distance between the fists.

3. Repeat the same test on the opposite side, right hand over the top.

4. Compare these numbers to your hand-length measurement. If either side is greater than your hand measure, you might have a shoulder mobility issue that should be addressed.

THE INTEGRATED STRENGTH SESSION FORMAT

Training sessions should be simple and logical to follow. We prefer to under-program the training and let athletes add-on more at the end than to over-program and risk them not finishing the workout. In the standard integrated strength sessions, we program three hangboard exercises, three strength exercises, and three mobility drills. These are grouped into small circuits that are each performed three times. For example, in one circuit, you'd do an edge hang, a set of squats, and a kneeling hip flexor stretch. This group would be done three times before moving on to the next group.

The pacing of this session is its beauty, you move slowly and deliberately between the three exercises, and the movements and loads are different enough that each exercise serves as an effective "rest" from the other two. For most climbers, each circuit takes about five minutes, and thus each group takes about fifteen. Including a good warm-up, the session takes about an hour. That being said, there is no reason to hurry through this...going heavy is more important than going fast.

The basic format looks like this:

3 ROUNDS, RESTING AS NEEDED
Hangboard Position 1
Hip Hinge
Hip Mobility

3 ROUNDS, RESTING AS NEEDED
Hangboard Position 2
Upper Body Press
Shoulder Mobility

3 ROUNDS, RESTING AS NEEDED
Hangboard Position 3
Squat
Hip Mobility

There is little reason to add more groups, rounds, or sets. The volume is high enough to make you stronger but low enough to keep from tapping you out for the week. If you need a little more work, consider adding some easy bouldering or route laps at the end of the session. If you are in the weight room (and can't climb right after the session), consider adding a barbell or kettlebell complex.

Below are three session formats we've used successfully with our athletes:

INTEGRATED STRENGTH 1 (10 SECOND HANGS)

This is a standard, easy-to-implement program that can be done in most good gyms.

3 ROUNDS, RESTING AS NEEDED
Open Hand Hang, 2 Arms x10 sec
Deadlift x3
Frog x60 sec

3 ROUNDS, RESTING AS NEEDED
Pinch Block, 3" x10 sec per side
One-Arm Overhead Press x6+6
Kettlebell Arm Bar x30 sec per side

3 ROUNDS, RESTING AS NEEDED
Half Crimp, 2 Arms x 10 sec
Pistol Squat x3+3
Tug of War Squat x 60 sec

INTEGRATED STRENGTH 2 (SINGLE-ARM HANGS, 10 SEC HANGS)

This workout implements the single-arm hangboard protocol with resistance and mobility training. This is a good program for an intermediate to advanced trainee.

3 ROUNDS, RESTING AS NEEDED
Half Crimp, 1 Arm, Straight Arm x10 sec per side
Kettlebell Swing x10
Frog x60 sec

3 ROUNDS, RESTING AS NEEDED
Half Crimp, 1 Arm, Bent Arm x10 sec per side
One-Arm Push-Up x6+6
Latissimus Traction 60 sec

3 ROUNDS, RESTING AS NEEDED
Half Crimp, 1 Arm, Lock Off x10 sec per side
Split Squat x3+3
Tug of War Squat x 60 sec

INTEGRATED STRENGTH 3 (BODYWEIGHT ONLY, 3-3-3 SECOND HANGS)

This workout is appropriate for those who do not have a weight room close to their hangboard. This session incorporates Go 30 hangboard plan with bodyweight resistance exercise.

3 ROUNDS, RESTING AS NEEDED
Half Crimp, 2 Arms, Straight Arm x 10 seconds
Single Leg Hip Thrust x10+10
Frog stretch x60 sec

3 ROUNDS, RESTING AS NEEDED
Pinch Block, 3" x 10 seconds
One-Arm Push-Up x3+3
Overhead Squat 60 sec

3 ROUNDS, RESTING AS NEEDED
Pocket Hang, Second Pair, 2 Arms, Straight Arm
x 10 seconds
Pistol Squat x3+3
Tug of War Squat x 60 sec

PROGRAMMING INTEGRATED STRENGTH

We do these sessions 2-3 days per week during a strength phase. In-season, climbers will use this as a strength-maintenance session every week or 10 days. This also works as an effective test: although you don't want to increase your loads in-season, you also don't want to regress. If you start to get weaker, it's probably time to up your high-load training again or train strength more frequently.

On a week-to-week basis, we program strength when it is going to be the least invasive - usually at the end of a climbing day or the day after climbing. Some example weeks are as follows:

BASE PHASE:

M	TU	W	TH	F	SA	SU
Integrated Strength		Integrated Strength		Integrated Strength		Climbing

BUILD PHASE:

M	TU	W	TH	F	SA	SU
Boulder/ Climb	Integrated Strength		Boulder/ Climb	Integrated Strength		Climbing

PERFORMANCE PHASE:

M	TU	W	TH	F	SA	SU
Climb RP		Climb RP	Integrated Strength		Climb RP	

The bottom line with programming is you want to train as little as possible to achieve the desired results. If you are getting stronger on three days a week, try backing off a bit and see if the gains still come. The mistake we make, that we all make, is thinking that we can somehow increase the slow process of adaptation by adding more training. Strength comes slowly.

CHAPTER 14

ONE LAST THING

PHOTO: ZACH SNAVELY

"

DO NOT PRAY FOR EASY LIVES. PRAY TO BE STRONGER MEN. DO NOT PRAY FOR TASKS EQUAL TO YOUR POWERS. PRAY FOR POWERS EQUAL TO YOUR TASKS."

PHILIPS BROOKS

The pursuit of easier, more comfortable jobs, lives, relationships, or rock climbs is a dangerous pursuit. It is in placing comfort as a goal that we no longer can find comfort, as if by looking for the thing it becomes invisible to us. The more days you stay in because it's cold, the more times you hang on the rope because you are pumped, the more times you turn from your fear, the more difficult things will be next time.

To pick up a weight is a vote against seeking comfort. Every time you move weight or hold on to small edges, you are pushing that comfort zone back. You are creating a better version of yourself that is more capable of today's tasks and will be better prepared for tomorrow's. The greatest reward we ever receive as strength coaches is the look on the faces of our athletes when they set new personal bests.

With this book and the information you now have, you have the tools to be a better, more durable climber. You have the tools to avoid injury and to extend your career. You can build the foundation upon which you can put forth your best climbing, and keep it up for years to come.

CHAPTER 16

ABOUT THE AUTHORS

PHOTO: ZACH SNAVELY

STEVE BECHTEL

Steve Bechtel is a veteran strength and performance coach. He has been an active climber and explorer for over 30 years, and has established hundreds of routes across the globe. Steve is the founder of Climb Strong, a training and coaching business, and is one of the founding directors of the Performance Climbing Coach program. Steve operates Elemental Performance + Fitness with his wife Ellen, in Lander, Wyoming. Elemental is a full-service training gym with a focus on rock climbing. Steve has written more than a dozen climbing guidebooks. This is his sixth book on training for climbing.

CHARLIE MANGANIELLO

Charlie is a janitor turned strength and climbing coach. Charlie first met Steve Bechtel in February 2011 when he took a job at Elemental Performance + Fitness working the front desk, cleaning floors, setting routes, folding towels, and selling memberships. Charlie, already kind of into climbing, started to learn how to actually train for his favorite sport by watching and asking questions anytime he got the chance. After lots of encouragement by Steve, a couple of kettlebell certifications, and lots of books on strength training, Charlie has become one of the resident strength coaches at Elemental and Climb Strong. Charlie is now a coach for Climb Strong, training athletes in Lander as well as remote athletes around the country. He also coaches a youth climbing team. This is his second book on training for climbing.

ACKNOWLEDGEMENTS

As with any big project, on the rock or off, there is a long list of people who worked tirelessly to make this book come to life. We have an amazing team at our day job: coaching athletes at Elemental Performance+Fitness and with Climb Strong. Our biggest thanks to Ellen Bechtel who is the glue behind Elemental and Climb Strong. Thank you for putting up with our long meetings as we sifted through the details of the book you now hold in your hand. More thanks to our coaches Emily Tilden, Alex Bridgewater, Amanda Sempert, and Kevin Wallingford for waking up extra early on Saturday mornings to be our exercise models and being the great coaches that you are. A special thanks to Amanda for lending her eagle eye on many rounds of edits.

Thank you Kian Stewart for your creative mind and making our book become a presentable work of art, instead of a shorthand mad scientist Google document.

A special thanks to Zach Snavely for all the exercise photos and a few chapter photos. Your work capturing hundreds of photos through many sessions and then paring them down to the ones for this book is nothing short of amazing.

Photographers whose work appears in this book include Mei Ratz, Sam Lightner, Jr., Matt Enlow, Nate Liles, and Ryan Ferrian. Thanks for breaking up our dense text with inspiring photos.

Even though this felt like a totally new book, this is technically the second edition of Steve's original strength book. We are constantly learning, adapting, and modifying to bring you the most up-to-date and effective strength training protocols.

Thank you to all the athletes we coach in person, remotely, at conferences, and through passing. We are honored to coach you and thanks for being our test subjects. We are lucky to consult with and learn from the best in the sport, including Neely Quinn, Mike Anderson, Mark Anderson, Dr. Tyler Nelson, Dr. Jared Vagy, Kris Hampton, Chris Neve, Ken Klein, Justen Sjong, Zahan Billimoria, Kelly Drager, and Bradley Hilbert.

A very special thanks to our athletes who train and climb with us in Lander, Wyoming. The true lab rats include Mike Lilygren, Anne Peick, Anna Haegel, Kristin Anderson, Dennis Van Denbos, Kristen Lovelace, Tova Sulraz, Kathryn Perkinson, Emily Chien, Patrick Mcheyser, Jim Margolis, Liz Tuohy, and many more.

Behind every send, there are great belayers or spotters. In the case of this book, we said "take" many times. Thank you!

"One thousand days of lessons for discipline;

Ten thousand days of lessons for mastery."

MIYAMOTO MUSASHI